Holt McDougal

Geometry

Larson   Boswell   Kanold   Stiff

Using the Geometry Remediation Book

The Geometry Remediation Book is separated into six major subdivisions that help mark progress through the course. Each major subdivision is broken into 4 or 5 major topics. Each major topic contains 3 to 7 half page lessons, and a quiz that assesses the student's understanding. The lesson provides examples, vocabulary, helpful hints, and exercises.

HOLT McDOUGAL

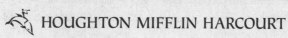
HOUGHTON MIFFLIN HARCOURT

COMMON CORE

EDITION

Printed in the U.S.A

ISBN 978-0-54771071-6

1 2 3 4 5 6 7 8 9 10   1421   20 19 18 17 16 15 14 13 12 11

4500307840   ^ B C D E F G

Contents

BENCHMARK 1
(Chapters 1 and 2)

A. Line Segments

In geometry, the words point, line and plane are undefined terms. They do not have formal definitions but there is agreement about what they mean. Terms that can be described using these words, such as line segment and ray, are called defined terms. The formal definitions allow us to calculate the length and midpoint of a line segment.

1. Name Points, Lines, Segments, and Rays

Vocabulary

The **line segment** $\overline{AB}$ consists of all points on the line $\overleftrightarrow{AB}$ that are between A and B.

The **ray** $\overrightarrow{AB}$ consists of the endpoint A and all points on the line $\overleftrightarrow{AB}$ which lie on the same side of A as B.

EXAMPLE   **Use the diagram to name points, lines, and line segments.**

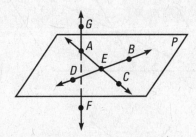

a. Name two line segments in line $\overleftrightarrow{AC}$.

Ray $\overrightarrow{AB}$ is in plane P even though it is not drawn in.

b. Name three points in P which are not collinear.

c. Name a ray which is not in plane P.

d. Name a point which is on line $\overleftrightarrow{GF}$ and ray $\overrightarrow{CE}$.

Solution:

a. $\overline{AC}$ and $\overline{EA}$, for example

b. A, E, B is one possibility

c. $\overrightarrow{AG}$ or $\overrightarrow{AF}$

d. A

PRACTICE   **Use the diagram.**

1. Give another name to plane Q.

2. Give three different names for $\overleftrightarrow{DF}$.

3. Name three points which are collinear.

4. Are $\overline{DE}$ and $\overline{ED}$ the same line segment?

5. Are $\overrightarrow{GC}$ and $\overrightarrow{CG}$ the same ray?

6. Name two pairs of opposite rays.

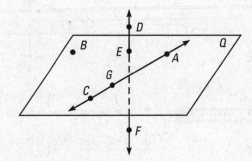

BENCHMARK 1
(Chapters 1 and 2)

2. Sketch Intersections

The **intersection** of two or more geometric figures is the set of points the figures have in common.

EXAMPLE **a.** Sketch two intersecting lines and the plane that they determine.

b. Sketch three lines such that each pair intersects in a point which is not on the line which remains.

c. Sketch a pair of lines which do not intersect and which are not contained in the same plane.

Solution:

a.

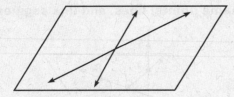

b.

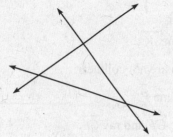

c.

A dashed line in a diagram indicates the line is out of view.

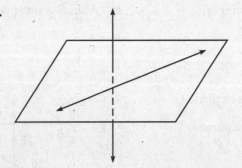

7. Draw two rays whose intersection is a point.

8. Draw two rays whose intersection is a line segment.

BENCHMARK 1
(Chapters 1 and 2)

9. Draw two rays whose intersection is a ray.

10. Draw two lines which do not intersect and which are contained in the same plane.

11. Draw two lines which do not intersect but which are contained in planes that do intersect.

12. Is it possible for three planes to intersect in just a single point? Explain.

3. Find Lengths of Line Segments

Vocabulary

The line segments $\overline{AB}$ and $\overline{CD}$ are **congruent** if they have the same length; that is, if $AB = CD$. We write $\overline{AB} \cong \overline{CD}$ to denote congruence.

EXAMPLE $J(2, 2)$, $K(2, -3)$, $L(-1, 3)$, and $M(4, 3)$ are plotted in the coordinate plane below.

a. Is $\overline{JK}$ congruent to $\overline{LM}$?

b. Is $\overline{LJ}$ congruent to $\overline{JM}$?

c. Is $\overline{JM}$ congruent to $\overline{KM}$?

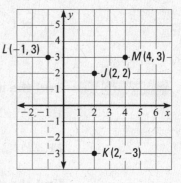

$\overline{AB} \neq AB$
The left hand side is a set of points while the right hand side is a number.

Solution:

a. Yes, we can see that each segment has length 5.

b. We measure and see that, no, $\overline{LJ}$ and $\overline{JM}$ do not have the same length.

c. We measure and see that, no, $\overline{JM}$ and $\overline{KM}$ do not have the same length.

PRACTICE   **Use the diagram.**

13. Name a segment which is half as long as $\overline{AC}$.

14. Could $DA = 4$?

15. Which segment is congruent to $\overline{DE}$?

16. Which segment has length $2(EO)$?

17. Name two pairs of congruent line segments.

18. Is it true that $AO + OC = AC$?

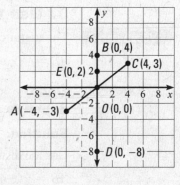

BENCHMARK 1
(Chapters 1 and 2)

4. Use the Midpoint Formula

Vocabulary

The **midpoint of a line segment** with endpoints (x_1, y_1) and (x_2, y_2) has coordinates $\left(\dfrac{x_1 + x_2}{2}, \dfrac{y_1 + y_2}{2}\right)$.

EXAMPLE

a. The endpoints of $\overline{AB}$ are $A(2, -3)$ and $B(-4, 6)$. Find the coordinates of the midpoint, M.

b. The midpoint of $\overline{CD}$ is $M(2, 4)$. One endpoint is $C(0, -1)$. Find the coordinates of D.

Think of the coordinates of the midpoint of a segment as the averages of the coordinates of the endpoints of the segment.

Solution:

a. M has x-coordinate $\dfrac{2 + (-4)}{2} = -1$ and y-coordinate $\dfrac{-3 + 6}{2} = \dfrac{3}{2}$.

The coordinates of the midpoint are $M\left(-1, \dfrac{3}{2}\right)$.

b. The x-coordinate of D satisfies $\dfrac{x + 0}{2} = 2$ so that x must be 4. The y-coordinate of D satisfies $\dfrac{y + (-1)}{2} = 4$ so that y must be 9. The coordinates of D are $(4, 9)$.

PRACTICE

Find the midpoint of $\overline{PQ}$ using the given coordinates.

19. $P(2, 2)$ and $Q(3, 3)$

20. $P(-2, 0)$ and $Q(5, -3)$

21. $P(1.2, 8)$ and $Q(3.5, -6.1)$

22. $P\left(\dfrac{3}{5}, 2\right)$ and $Q\left(-1, \dfrac{4}{3}\right)$

Find the coordinates of S if the midpoint of RS is M.

23. $R(-6, 4)$ and $M\left(-\dfrac{3}{2}, 3\right)$

24. $R(5, -1)$ and $M\left(\dfrac{1}{2}, -\dfrac{9}{2}\right)$

5. Use the Distance Formula

Vocabulary

The **distance** between points $A(x_1, y_1)$ and $B(x_2, y_2)$ is given by the distance formula $AB = \sqrt{(x_2 - x_1)^2 + (y_2 - y_1)^2}$.

EXAMPLE

Find the length of $\overline{AB}$ if the endpoints are $A(2, -3)$ and $B(-4, 6)$. Round to the nearest tenth of a unit.

Solution:

Use the distance formula.

$AB = \sqrt{(-4 - 2)^2 + [6 - (-3)]^2} = \sqrt{36 + 81} = \sqrt{117} \approx 10.8$

PRACTICE

Find the length of segment using the coordinates indicated. Round to the nearest tenth of a unit

To remember the distance formula, think of the Pythagorean Theorem.

25. $P(2, 2)$ and $Q(3, 3)$

26. $P(-2, 0)$ and $Q(5, -3)$

27. $P(1.2, 8)$ and $Q(3.5, -6.1)$

28. $P\left(\dfrac{3}{5}, 2\right)$ and $Q\left(-1, \dfrac{4}{3}\right)$

29. $P(-4, 0)$ and $Q(4, 0)$

30. $P(-a, 2)$ and $Q(a, 2)$

BENCHMARK 1
(Chapters 1 and 2)

Quiz
Use the diagram.

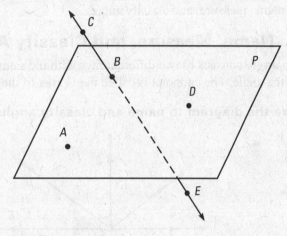

1. Give another name for plane *P*.

2. What is the intersection of $\overleftrightarrow{BC}$ with the plane *P*?

3. Name a point not on line $\overleftrightarrow{AB}$.

4. What is the intersection of $\overrightarrow{CE}$ with $\overrightarrow{BC}$?

The endpoints of three line segments are *A*(1, 5), *B*(3, −1), and *C*(7, 3).

5. Find the midpoint of $\overline{BC}$.

6. Find the exact length of $\overline{AC}$.

7. Find the exact length of $\overline{AB}$.

8. Is $\overline{AB} \cong \overline{AC}$?

BENCHMARK 1
(Chapters 1 and 2)

B. Angles

An angle can be acute, obtuse, or right. In the examples which follow, we describe how to name, measure, and classify angles.

1. Name, Measure, and Classify Angles

Vocabulary An **angle** consists of two different rays with the same endpoint. The rays are the **sides** of the angle. The endpoint is called the **vertex** of the angle.

EXAMPLE **Use the diagram to name and classify angles.**

Angles can be measured in degrees or radians. We are using degrees here.

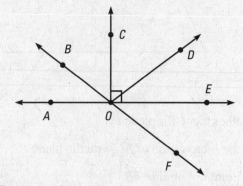

   a. Name two acute angles.

   b. Name three obtuse angles.

   c. Name four right angles (use your protractor to be sure).

   d. Give another name for $\angle BOC$.

Solution:

   a. $\angle BOC$ and $\angle EOF$, for example

   b. $\angle AOD$, $\angle BOE$, and $\angle COF$ are all obtuse angles

   c. $\angle AOC$ and $\angle COE$ are right angles

   d. $\angle COB$

PRACTICE **Use the diagram.**

   1. Give two different names for $\angle ABC$.

   2. Name two straight angles.

   3. Use a protractor to measure $\angle CDG$ and $\angle FAH$.

   4. Do there appear to be any right angles?

   5. How many obtuse angles are shown in the diagram?

   6. How many acute angles are shown in the diagram?

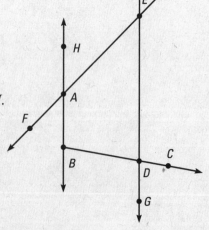

Name _____ Date _____

BENCHMARK 1
(Chapters 1 and 2)

2. Find Angle Measures

Vocabulary

The **bisector of an angle** is a ray that divides the angle into two angles which have the same measure.

EXAMPLE

Every angle has exactly one bisector.

Use the diagram to find angle measures.

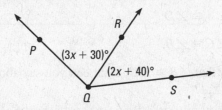

a. If $m\angle PQS = 85°$, what is $m\angle PQR$ and $m\angle RQS$?

b. What is the value of x if $\overrightarrow{QR}$ bisects $\angle PQS$?

Solution:

a. We must have that $(3x + 30) + (2x + 40) = 85$ so that $x = 3$. This means that $m\angle PQR = [3(3) + 30]° = 39°$ and $m\angle RQS = [2(3) + 40]° = 46°$.

b. We must have that $3x + 30 = 2x + 40$ so that $x = 10$.

PRACTICE **Use the diagram.**

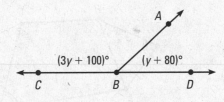

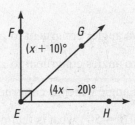

7. Is $\angle FEG$ acute?

8. Find the value of x.

9. Does $\overrightarrow{EG}$ bisect $\angle FEH$?

10. Could $\angle CBA$ and $\angle ABD$ both be obtuse?

11. Find the value of y.

12. Does $\overrightarrow{BA}$ bisect $\angle CBD$?

BENCHMARK 1
(Chapters 1 and 2)

3. Identify Congruent Angles

Vocabulary $\angle A$ is **congruent** to $\angle B$ if $m\angle A = m\angle B$. We write $\angle A \cong \angle B$ to denote congruence of angles.

EXAMPLE

$\angle A \neq m\angle A$.

The left hand side is a set of points, the right hand side is a number.

The diagram shows two lines intersecting in a point.

a. Show that $\angle A \cong \angle D$.

b. Show that $\angle C \cong \angle B$.

c. If you know that $\angle B \cong \angle D$, what can you say about the measure of $\angle A$?

Solution:

a. Since $m\angle A + m\angle C = 180°$ and $m\angle D + m\angle C = 180°$, we must have that $m\angle A = m\angle D$ so that $\angle A \cong \angle D$.

b. Since $m\angle A + m\angle C = 180°$ and $m\angle A + m\angle B = 180°$, we must have that $m\angle C = m\angle B$ so that $\angle C \cong \angle B$.

c. If $\angle B \cong \angle D$, then $m\angle B = m\angle D$. Thus, $m\angle B = 90°$, since $m\angle B + m\angle D = 180°$. Since $m\angle A + m\angle B = 180°$, we must have that $m\angle A = 90°$ as well.

PRACTICE   **Use the diagram.**

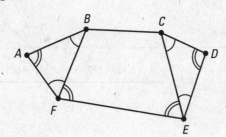

13. Name two angles congruent to $\angle A$.

14. Name two angles congruent to $\angle ECD$.

15. Name an angle which is congruent to $\angle AFE$.

16. If $m\angle AFB = 50°$, what is the measure of $\angle DCE$?

17. Suppose that $m\angle ABC = 150°$ and $m\angle DCB = 150°$. What can we say about $\angle FBC$ and $\angle ECB$?

18. If $m\angle CEF = (2x + 50)°$ and $m\angle FAB = (4x + 20)°$, what is the value of x?

BENCHMARK 1
(Chapters 1 and 2)

4. Find Measures of a Complement and a Supplement

Vocabulary

Two angles are **complementary angles** if the sum of their measures is 90°. Two angles are **supplementary angles** if the sum of their measures is 180°. Two angles are **adjacent angles** if they have a common vertex and side but no common interior points.

EXAMPLE

A complement "completes" a right angle.

a. Given that $\angle A$ is a complement of $\angle B$ and that $m\angle A = 57°$, what is $m\angle B$?

b. Given that $\angle C$ is a supplement of $\angle D$ and that $m\angle C = 105°$, what is $m\angle D$?

Solution:

a. Since $m\angle A + m\angle B = 90°$, we have that $57° + m\angle B = 90°$ so that $m\angle B = 33°$.

b. Since $m\angle C + m\angle D = 180°$, we have that $105° + m\angle D = 180°$ so that $m\angle D = 75°$.

PRACTICE

Given that $\angle E$ and $\angle F$ are complementary and that $\angle G$ and $\angle H$ are supplementary, find $m\angle F$ and $m\angle H$ in each case.

19. $m\angle E = 30°$, $m\angle G = 30°$

20. $m\angle E = 42°$, $m\angle G = 120°$

21. $m\angle E = 18.5°$, $m\angle G = 125.2°$

22. $m\angle E = 45°$, $m\angle G = 90°$

23. $m\angle E = 60°$, $m\angle G = 45°$

24. $m\angle E = 89°$, $m\angle G = 60°$

5. Find Angle Measures in a Linear Pair

Vocabulary

Two angles form a **linear pair** if they are adjacent and their non-common sides are opposite rays. The angles in a linear pair are supplementary. Two angles are **vertical angles** if their sides form two pairs of opposite rays.

EXAMPLE

One angle in a linear pair "supplements" the other to form a line.

Identify all of the linear pairs and all of the vertical angles labeled in the figure below.

Solution:

To find linear pairs, look for adjacent angles whose noncommon sides are opposite rays: $\angle 1$ and $\angle 2$ are a linear pair.

To find vertical angles, look for angles formed by intersecting lines: $\angle 2$ and $\angle 5$ are vertical angles.

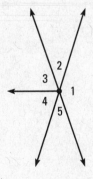

BENCHMARK 1
(Chapters 1 and 2)

PRACTICE   Refer to the figure below.

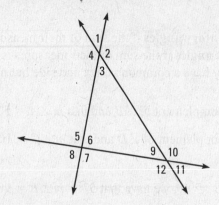

25. Name a vertical pair containing ∠4.

26. Which two angles each form a linear pair with ∠1?

27. Name a vertical pair containing ∠8.

28. Which two angles each form a linear pair with ∠12?

Quiz

Lines $\overleftrightarrow{AC}$ and $\overleftrightarrow{FE}$ intersect in point B in the diagram.

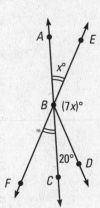

1. Name a pair of obtuse vertical angles.

2. Identify a linear pair.

3. Give another name for ∠FBC.

4. Find the value of x.

5. What is $m\angle DBE$?

6. Name a pair of supplementary angles which are not a linear pair.

7. One angle in the diagram is bisected by a ray. Name that angle and that ray.

8. Name a pair of congruent angles.

BENCHMARK 1
(Chapters 1 and 2)

C. Polygons

A **polygon** is a closed plane figure which is formed by three or more line segments, called sides. Each side intersects exactly two other sides, one at each endpoint, so that no two sides with a common endpoint are collinear.

While a circle is not a polygon, it can be thought of as a regular *n*-gon where *n* is infinite.

1. Identify Polygons

Vocabulary

A polygon is **convex** if no line that contains a side of the polygon also contains a point in the interior of the polygon. A polygon which is not convex is called **concave** or **nonconvex**.

EXAMPLE   **Tell whether each figure is a polygon and, if it is a polygon, tell whether it is convex or concave.**

a.

b.

c.
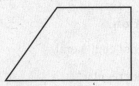

d.
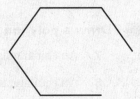

Solution:

a. Some of the line segments intersect more than two other segments, so it is not a polygon.

b. The figure is a concave polygon.

c. The figure is a convex polygon.

d. The figure has sides which intersect only one other side, so it is not a polygon.

PRACTICE   **Draw a polygon that fits the description.**

1. Three-sided and convex

2. Four-sided and convex

3. Four-sided and concave

4. Five-sided and convex

5. Five-sided and concave

6. Eight-sided and convex

BENCHMARK 1
(Chapters 1 and 2)

2. Classify Polygons

Vocabulary

An **equilateral polygon** has all its sides congruent to each other. An **equiangular polygon** has all its interior angles equal to each other. A **regular polygon** is both equilateral and equiangular.

EXAMPLE

A square is a regular quadrilateral.

Classify the polygon by the number of sides. Tell whether the polygon is equilateral, equiangular, or regular.

a.
b.
c.

Solution:

a. The polygon has 10 sides. It is equilateral, but not equiangular since not all of its interior angles are equal to each other. So this decagon is not regular.

b. This equilateral polygon has 4 sides all of equal length and all its interior angles are equal. It is a regular quadrilateral.

c. This 3 sided polygon, a triangle, is not regular because it is neither equilateral nor equiangular.

PRACTICE

Draw a polygon that fits the description.

7. An equiangular quadrilateral which is not equilateral.

8. An equilateral quadrilateral which is not regular.

9. A regular heptagon.

10. A concave equilateral nonagon.

11. A concave heptagon which is not regular.

12. A convex equiangular pentagon.

3. Find Circumference and Area of a Circle.

Vocabulary

Pi, or π, is the ratio of a circle's circumference to its diameter.

EXAMPLE

Remember how π is defined. It is *not* actually 3.14.

You are ordering a circular tablecloth for your grandmother's oak table. Find the approximate circumference and area of the tablecloth shown.

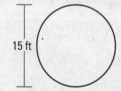

15 ft

BENCHMARK 1
(Chapters 1 and 2)

Solution:

First find the radius. The diameter is 15 feet, so the radius is

$\frac{1}{2}(15) = 7.5$ feet. Then find the circumference and area.

Use 3.14 to approximate the value of π.

$C = 2\pi r \approx 2(3.14)(7.5) = 47.1$ and $A = \pi r^2 \approx 3.14(7.5)^2 = 176.6$

Thus, the circumference is about 47.1 feet and the area is about 176.6 square feet.

PRACTICE   **Find the circumference and area of a circle with the given radius. Round to the nearest tenth.**

13. $r = 15$ cm   **14.** $r = 12$ miles   **15.** $r = 125$ m

16. $r = 21.8$ in.   **17.** $r = 3$ yd   **18.** $r = 30$ ft

Quiz

Classify the polygon shown. Be as descriptive as you can.

1.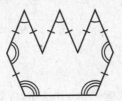

2.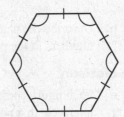

3.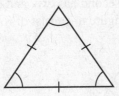

4.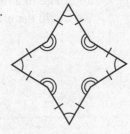

Find the circumference and area of the circles. Round to the nearest tenth.

5.

8 ft

6.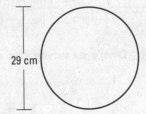

29 cm

BENCHMARK 1
(Chapters 1 and 2)

D. Inductive and Deductive Reasoning

Humans have different ways of thinking. We may intuitively know something without reasoning it out step by step. For example, we can often predict the next term in a given pattern. When we do this, we are using inductive reasoning. While such reasoning is highly important and gives us insight into a situation, we require deductive reasoning to justify the conclusions that we make.

1. Describe a Pattern

Vocabulary

A **pattern** is a sequence of objects that can be recognized by some rule.

EXAMPLE

It is not always possible to determine the next object of a pattern.

a. Describe how to sketch the fourth figure in the pattern.

b. Describe the pattern in the numbers 1, −2, 3, −4, … and write the next three numbers in the pattern.

Solution:

a. Each figure consists of a collection of lines such that every pair of lines intersects in a point but there is no point which is common to three or more lines. The first figure has one line, the second has two, and the third has three. We would therefore expect the fourth figure to consist of four such lines:

b. The numbers alternate from positive to negative values and the absolute value of the first term is 1, the absolute value of the second term is 2, the absolute value of the third term is three, and so on. Thus we would expect the next three terms to be 5, −6, and 7.

PRACTICE

Draw or write the next object in the pattern.

1. a, e, i, …

2. →, ↓, ←, …

3. ⊗, ⊗⊗, ⊗⊗⊗, …

4. ⌈, ⌉, ⊔, ⊔, ▶, ◀, ⊓ …

5. 1, 4, 9, 16, 25, …

6. 1, 1, 2, 3, 5, 8, …

7. abcde, bcdea, cdeab, …

8. Tuesday, Sunday, Friday, Wednesday, …

BENCHMARK 1
(Chapters 1 and 2)

2. Make and Test a Conjecture

Vocabulary

A **conjecture** is an unproven statement that is based on observations. You use **inductive reasoning** when you find a pattern in specific cases and then write a conjecture for the general case.

EXAMPLE

Make and test a conjecture about the product of two consecutive numbers.

Solution:

A conjecture is an educated guess.

Step 1: Find a pattern using a few pairs of consecutive numbers:

$1 \times 2 = 2$ $2 \times 3 = 6$ $3 \times 4 = 12$ $4 \times 5 = 20$

We conjecture that the product of any two consecutive numbers is even.

Step 2: Test the conjecture using other numbers:

$153 \times 154 = 23{,}562$ $1000 \times 1001 = 1{,}001{,}000$

PRACTICE

9. Make and test a conjecture about the product of any number and zero.

10. Suppose 6 people are to be seated in a row. Make a conjecture about the number of different seating arrangements there are.

11. Suppose you are given 5 points in a plane. Make a conjecture about the maximum number of lines these points can determine.

12. Make and test a conjecture about the sum of the digits of a number and whether or not that number is divisible by 3.

3. Find a Counterexample

Vocabulary

A **counterexample** is a specific case for which a conjecture is false.

EXAMPLE

A student makes a conjecture about products and sums. Find a counterexample to disprove the student's conjecture.

One counterexample is enough to disprove a conjecture.

Conjecture: The product of any two numbers is always greater than their sum.

Solution:

To find a counterexample, we seek two numbers whose product is smaller than the sum of those numbers. We try -1 and 2:

$-1 \times 2 = -2$ $-1 + 2 = 1$ -2 is not greater than 1

Because a counterexample to the conjecture exists, the conjecture is false.

PRACTICE

13. Suppose your friend claims that every car in the school parking lot is red, and you wish to prove him wrong by presenting him with a counterexample. Describe what you should be looking for.

14. Find a counterexample to show that the following conjecture is false: "The value of $\frac{1}{x}$ is smaller than the value of x whenever $x > 0$."

BENCHMARK 1
(Chapters 1 and 2)

15. Suppose Viktor is a counterexample to the conjecture, "All red-headed boys have green eyes and freckles." What must be true about Viktor?

16. Provide a counterexample to the conjecture, "If the product of two numbers is 1, then at least one of the numbers must be 1."

4. Write Four Related Conditional Statements

Vocabulary There are four **conditional statements** we can form. **If-then:** "If A then B."
Converse: "If B then A." **Inverse:** "If not A then not B." **Contrapositive:** "If not B then not A."

EXAMPLE **Write the if-then, converse, inverse, and contrapositive of the conditional statement "Cows are mammals." Decide whether each statement is *true* or *false*.**

Solution:

The four related statements are similar but have very different meanings.

If-then form "If you are a cow, then you are a mammal." True. Cows are mammals.

Converse form "If you are a mammal, then you are a cow." False. You and I are mammals but we are not cows.

Inverse form "If you are not a cow, then you are not a mammal." False. Even if you are not a cow, you could still be a mammal.

Contrapositive "If you are not a mammal, then you are not a cow." True. An animal which is not a mammal cannot be a cow.

PRACTICE **Write the converse, inverse, and contrapositive of each given conditional statement, and tell whether each statement is *true* or *false*.**

17. If a number is even, then it is an integer.

18. If it rains, then I will open my umbrella.

19. If n and m are both even, then $n + m$ is even.

5. Write a Biconditional Statement

Vocabulary A **biconditional statement** contains the phrase "if and only if."

EXAMPLE **Write the definition of positive number as a biconditional.**

The phrase "if and only if" is so common in mathematics it is often abbreviated as "iff."

Solution:

Definition If a number is positive, then it is greater than zero.

Converse If a number is greater than zero, then it is positive.

Biconditional A number is positive if and only if it is greater than zero.

PRACTICE **20.** Rewrite the definition of complementary angles as a biconditional statement.

21. Rewrite the definition of angle bisector as a biconditional statement.

22. Rewrite the following two statements as a single biconditional: "If I work, I am paid. If I am paid, I work."

BENCHMARK 1
(Chapters 1 and 2)

6. Use the Laws of Detachment and Syllogism

Vocabulary

The **law of detachment** states that if the hypothesis of a true conditional statement is true then the conclusion is also true. The **law of syllogism** states that if the statement "If A then B." is true and the statement "If B then C." is true, then the statement "If A then C." is also true.

EXAMPLE

a. Use the Law of Detachment to make a valid conclusion in the following true situation: "Bertha goes to church every Sunday. Today is Sunday."

The law of detachment is also known as "modus ponens."

b. If possible, use the Law of Syllogism to write the conditional statement which follows from the pair of true statements: "If $\sin x = 0$ then x is a multiple of π. If x is a multiple of π, then x is irrational."

Solution:

a. Since "Today is Sunday" satisfies the hypothesis of the conditional statement, you can conclude that Bertha will go to church today.

b. The conclusion of the first statement is the hypothesis of the second, so you can write the following statement: "If $\sin x = 0$ then x is irrational."

PRACTICE

Use the Law of Detachment to make a valid conclusion.

23. If A is between B and C, then $BA + AC = BC$. A is between B and C.

24. Three noncollinear points determine a plane. A, B, and C are noncollinear.

Use the Law of Syllogism to write the conditional statement which follows from the pair of true statements.

25. If I am sad, I cry. If I cry, my nose runs.

26. If we go bowling, we will have fun. If I do my homework, we will go bowling.

Quiz

1. Write the next number in the pattern:

$$1, -\frac{1}{3}, \frac{1}{9}, -\frac{1}{27}, \cdots$$

2. Suppose 4 people shake hands. Make a conjecture about how many handshakes are made.

3. Give a counterexample which disproves the conjecture, "If $x^2 = 4$ then $x = 2$."

4. Write the 4 conditional statements related to the assertion, "All dogs bark."

5. Write the definition of midpoint as a biconditional statement.

6. Use the Law of Detachment to make a valid conclusion from the true statement, "If $m\angle A < 90°$, then $\angle A$ is acute. $m\angle A < 90°$."

7. Does the Law of Syllogism apply to the following pair of statements? "If a polygon is regular, then it is convex. If a polygon is regular, then it is equilateral."

BENCHMARK 1
(Chapters 1 and 2)

E. Writing Proofs

A **proof** is a logical argument that shows a statement is true. There are many different formats for proving mathematical truths. We focus on the two-column proof.

1. Identify Postulates

Vocabulary   A **postulate** or **axiom** is a rule which is accepted without proof. Several postulates have been presented in your book so far. A **theorem** is a rule which has been proven.

EXAMPLE   **a.** State the postulate illustrated by the diagram.

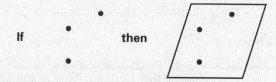

Theorems are proven; postulates are accepted without proof.

b. Use the diagram to write an example of Postulate 6.

Solution:

a. Postulate 8: Through any three noncollinear points there exists exactly one plane.

b. Postulate 6: Line ℓ contains at least two points, A and B.

PRACTICE   **State the postulate illustrated by the diagram.**

1.

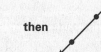

2.

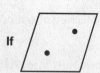

Use the diagram to write an example of the given postulate

3. Postulate 11

4. Postulate 7

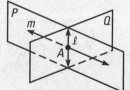

BENCHMARK 1
(Chapters 1 and 2)

2. Sketch a Diagram

Vocabulary **A line is perpendicular to a plane** if and only if the line intersects the plane in a point and is perpendicular to every line in the plane that intersects it at that point.

EXAMPLE **Sketch a diagram showing $\overleftrightarrow{TV}$ intersecting plane P at point W so that $\overleftrightarrow{TV}$ is perpendicular to P and W is the midpoint of $\overline{TV}$.**

Solution:

Be sure to include the small square symbol in your diagrams to indicate perpendicularity.

Step 1: Draw P and label it. Draw point W in P and label it.

Step 2: Draw $\overleftrightarrow{TV}$ through W so that it appears perpendicular to P. Include the right angle symbol.

Step 3: Label points T and V on the line so that W is the midpoint of $\overline{TV}$. Mark the segments $\overline{TW}$ and $\overline{WV}$ as congruent.

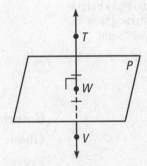

PRACTICE 5. Sketch a diagram showing $\overrightarrow{BD}$ bisecting $\angle ABC$.

6. Sketch a diagram showing $\angle ABC$ and $\angle CBD$ as a linear pair contained in plane P.

7. Sketch a diagram showing $\overleftrightarrow{AB}$ perpendicular to plane P at point A and perpendicular to plane R at point B.

8. Sketch a diagram showing $\angle CDB$ with point A in its interior so that $\overline{CA} \cong \overline{BA}$.

3. Use Properties of Equality

Vocabulary Let a, b, and c be real numbers. **Addition Property:** If $a = b$ then $a + c = b + c$. **Subtraction Property:** If $a = b$ then $a - c = b - c$. **Multiplication Property:** If $a = b$ then $ac = bc$. **Division Property:** If $a = b$ and $c \neq 0$ then $\frac{a}{c} = \frac{b}{c}$. **Substitution Property:** If $a = b$ then a can be substituted for b in any equation or expression. **Distributive Property:** $a(b + c) = ab + ac$.

EXAMPLE **Solve $5(7x - 3) = 20$. Write a reason for each step.**

Solution:

Remember: Division by 0 is undefined!

Equation	Explanation	Reason
$5(7x - 3) = 20$	Write original equation.	Given
$35x - 15 = 20$	Multiply.	Distributive Property
$35x = 35$	Add 15 to each side.	Addition Property
$x = 1$	Divide each side by 35.	Division Property

PRACTICE **Solve each equation and write a reason for each step.**

9. $2x + 3 = 7$ 10. $-2 + x = 12 - 3x$

11. $3(x + 1) = 9$ 12. $4(2x + 6) = -3(8 + x)$

BENCHMARK 1
(Chapters 1 and 2)

4. Write a Two-Column Proof

Vocabulary A **two-column proof** has numbered statements and corresponding reasons that show an argument in logical order.

EXAMPLE

Think through your argument carefully before starting to write your proof.

Write a two-column proof to show that vertical angles are congruent. The situation is depicted in the diagram.

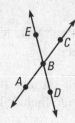

Solution:

Given: $\angle EBC$ and $\angle ABD$ are vertical angles.

Prove: $\angle EBC \cong \angle ABD$

Statements	Reasons
1. $\angle EBC$ and $\angle ABD$ are vertical.	**1.** Given
2. $m\angle ABC = 180°$	**2.** $\angle ABC$ is a straight angle.
3. $m\angle ABE + m\angle EBC = m\angle ABC$	**3.** Angle Addition Postulate
4. $m\angle ABE + m\angle EBC = 180°$	**4.** Substitution Property of Equality
5. $m\angle DBE = 180°$	**5.** $\angle BDE$ is a straight angle.
6. $m\angle ABD + m\angle ABE = \angle DBE$	**6.** Angle Addition Postulate
7. $m\angle ABD + m\angle ABE = 180°$	**7.** Substitution Property of Equality
8. $m\angle ABE + m\angle EBC = m\angle ABD + m\angle ABE$	**8.** Substitution Property of Equality
9. $m\angle EBC = m\angle ABD$	**9.** Subtraction Property of Equality
10. $\angle EBC \cong \angle ABD$	**10.** Definition of congruent angles

BENCHMARK 1
(Chapters 1 and 2)

PRACTICE Several steps of a proof are shown. Fill in the missing steps.

13. **Given:** $AC = AB + AB + AB$

   Prove : $AB = \frac{1}{2}BC$

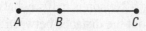

A ____●____ B ____●____ C

Statements	Reasons
1. $AC = AB + AB + AB$	1. Given
2. $AB + BC = AC$	2.
3. $AB + AB + AB = AB + BC$	3.
4. $AB + AB = BC$	4.
5. $2AB = BC$	5. Distributive Property
6. $AB = \frac{1}{2}BC$	6.

5. Prove a Statement About Segments

EXAMPLE Prove this property about line segments: If you know that **M** is the midpoint of $\overline{AB}$ and that **N** is the midpoint of $\overline{AN}$, prove that **AB** is four times **AN** and **AN** is one quarter **AB**.

A ●—— N ●—— M ●——————● B

Knowing your definitions will help you to write proofs.

Solution:

Given: M is the midpoint of $\overline{AB}$ and N is the midpoint of $\overline{AM}$

Prove: a. $4AN = AB$ and

   b. $AN = \frac{1}{4}AB$

Statements	Reasons
1. M is the midpoint of $\overline{AB}$ and N is the midpoint of $\overline{AM}$	1. Given
2. $\overline{AM} \cong \overline{MB}; \overline{AN} \cong \overline{NM}$	2. Definition of midpoint
3. $AM = MB; AN = NM$	3. Definition of congruent segments
4. $AM + MB = AB; AN + NM = AM$	4. Segment Addition Postulate
5. $AM + AM = AB; AN + AN = AM$	5. Substitution Property of Equality
6. $AN + AN + AN + AN = AB$	6. Substitution Property of Equality
7. $4AN = AB$	7. Distributive Property
8. $AN = \frac{1}{4}AB$	8. Division Property of Equality

BENCHMARK 1
(Chapters 1 and 2)

PRACTICE

14. Using the same givens as in previous example, write a two column proof

showing that $4NM = AB$ and $NM = \frac{1}{4}AB$.

15. Three towns, Alma, Nelson, and Winona are located along the same straight highway. If Nelson is halfway between Alma and Winona, what can you conclude about the distance between Alma and Nelson?

6. Use Theorems About Angles

EXAMPLE   **Use the diagram below to find the measure of an angle given that**
$m\angle AOB = m\angle BOC = m\angle FOE = 90°$.

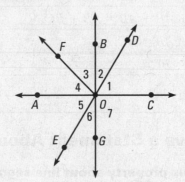

Read diagrams carefully. Do not assume anything that is not indicated.

a. If $m\angle 1 = 51°$ then find $m\angle 6$.   **b.** If $m\angle 6 = 32°$ then find $m\angle 4$.

c. If $m\angle 2 = 49°$ find $m\angle 3$.   **d.** If $m\angle 5 = 80°$ find $m\angle 1$.

Solution:

a. $m\angle 6 = m\angle 2 = 90° - m\angle 1 = 90° - 51° = 39°$.

b. $m\angle 4 + m\angle 5 = 90°$ and $m\angle 6 + m\angle 5 = 90°$ so $m\angle 4 = m\angle 6 = 32°$.

c. $m\angle 3 = 90° - m\angle 2 = 90° - 49° = 41°$.

d. $m\angle 1 = m\angle 5 = 80°$.

PRACTICE   **Use the diagram below to find the three remaining angle measures.**

16. If $m\angle 1 = 51°$ find $m\angle 2$, $m\angle 3$, and $m\angle 4$.

17. If $m\angle 2 = 149°$ find $m\angle 1$, $m\angle 3$, and $m\angle 4$.

18. If $m\angle 3 = 15°$ find $m\angle 1$, $m\angle 2$, and $m\angle 4$.

19. If $m\angle 4 = 135°$ find $m\angle 1$, $m\angle 2$, and $m\angle 3$.

BENCHMARK 1
(Chapters 1 and 2)

Quiz

1. Illustrate an example of Postulate 8 by drawing a diagram.

2. Sketch planes P, Q, and R intersecting in point M.

3. Solve the equation $9x + 3 = 21$ and give a reason for each step.

4. Write a two-column proof showing that if $\overrightarrow{AB}$ bisects $\angle CAD$ and $\overrightarrow{AE}$ bisects $\angle BAD$ then $m\angle CAD = 4m\angle EAD$.

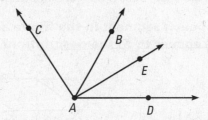

5. Find all the missing angle measures in the diagram below.

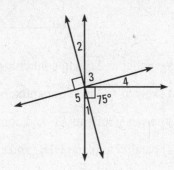

BENCHMARK 2
(Chapters 3 and 4)

A. Parallel and Perpendicular Lines

Two lines in the same plane either intersect in a point or are parallel. There are infinitely many lines through a point not on a given line. Exactly one of these lines is parallel to the given line, and exactly one of these lines is perpendicular to the given line.

1. Identify Relationships in Space

Vocabulary

Two lines are **parallel lines** if they do not intersect and are coplanar.

Two lines are **skew lines** if they do not intersect and are not coplanar.

EXAMPLE

Three lines drawn in a plane intersect in 0, 1, 2, or 3 points.

Think of each segment in the figure as part of a line. Which line(s) or plane(s) appear to fit the description?

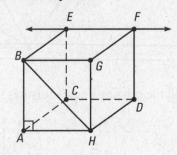

a. Line(s) parallel to $\overleftrightarrow{EF}$ and containing point B.

b. Line(s) skew to $\overleftrightarrow{EF}$ and containing point B.

c. Line(s) perpendicular to $\overleftrightarrow{EF}$ and containing point B.

d. Plane(s) parallel to plane HDC and containing point B.

Solution:

a. $\overleftrightarrow{BG}$ b. $\overleftrightarrow{BH}$ and $\overleftrightarrow{AB}$ c. $\overleftrightarrow{BE}$ d. Plane BEF

PRACTICE

Think of each segment in the figure as part of a line. Which line(s) or plane(s) appear to fit the description?

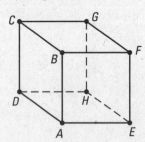

1. Line(s) parallel to $\overleftrightarrow{GH}$.

2. Line(s) parallel to $\overleftrightarrow{AE}$ containing point C.

3. Line(s) skew to $\overleftrightarrow{CB}$ containing point H.

4. Plane(s) parallel to plane CGD.

Name _____   Date _____

BENCHMARK 2
(Chapters 3 and 4)

2. Identify Angle Relationships

Vocabulary A **transversal** is a line that intersects two or more coplanar lines at different points. When two lines are cut by a transversal, there are four different kinds of pairs of angles formed: **corresponding, alternate interior, alternate exterior,** and **consecutive interior**.

EXAMPLE **Identify all pairs of angles of the given type.**

Practice identifying angle pairs.

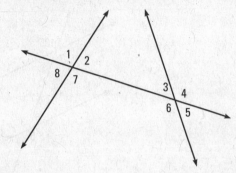

a. Corresponding

b. Alternate interior

c. Alternate exterior

d. Consecutive interior

Solution:

a. ∠1 and ∠3, ∠2 and ∠4, ∠8 and ∠6, ∠7 and ∠5

b. ∠2 and ∠6, ∠3 and ∠7

c. ∠1 and ∠5, ∠8 and ∠4

d. ∠2 and ∠3, ∠7 and ∠6

PRACTICE **Classify the pair of numbered angles.**

5.
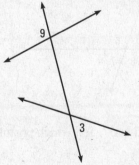

6.
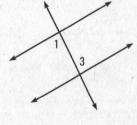

7.
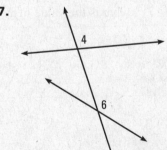

8.
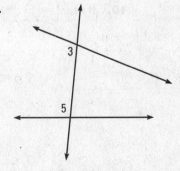

BENCHMARK 2
(Chapters 3 and 4)

3. Use Properties of Parallel Lines

Postulate The **Corresponding Angles Postulate** states that if two parallel lines are cut by a transversal then the pairs of corresponding angles are congruent.

EXAMPLE **The measure of three of the numbered angles is 135°. Identify the angles. Explain your reasoning.**

Don't assume a pair of lines are parallel or perpendicular based on appearances. Always justify your assumptions to yourself.

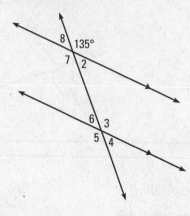

Solution:

By the Corresponding Angles Postulate, $m\angle 3 = 135°$. Using the Vertical Angles Congruence Theorem, $m\angle 7 = 135°$. Because $\angle 7$ and $\angle 5$ are corresponding angles, by the Corresponding Angles Postulate, $m\angle 5 = 135°$.

PRACTICE **Use the diagram.**

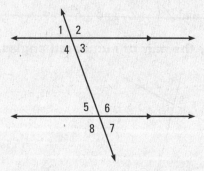

9. If $m\angle 1 = 40°$, find $m\angle 3$, $m\angle 5$, and $m\angle 7$. Tell which postulate or theorem you use in each case.

10. If $m\angle 2 = 137°$ and $m\angle 7 = (5x - 7)°$, what is the value of x?

BENCHMARK 2
(Chapters 3 and 4)

4. Prove Lines are Parallel

Vocabulary   The statements and reasons in a **paragraph proof** are written in sentences, using words to explain the logical flow of the argument.

Theorem   The converses of several theorems will help us prove arguments involving parallel lines:

The **Corresponding Angles Converse** states that if two lines are cut by a transversal so the corresponding angles are congruent, then the lines are parallel.

The **Alternate Interior Angles Converse** states that if two lines are cut by a transversal so the alternate interior angles are congruent, then the lines are parallel.

The **Alternate Exterior Angles Converse** states that if two lines are cut by a transversal so the alternate exterior angles are congruent, then the lines are parallel.

The **Consecutive Interior Angles Converse** states that if two lines are cut by a transversal so the consecutive interior angles are supplementary, then the lines are parallel.

EXAMPLE   **In the figure, $\ell \parallel m$ and $\angle 2$ is congruent to $\angle 4$. Prove that $p \parallel q$.**

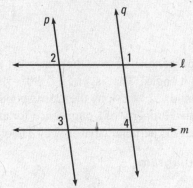

Use complete sentences and proper grammar when writing a proof.

Solution:

It is given that $\ell \parallel m$ so by the Corresponding Angles Postulate $\angle 2 \cong \angle 3$. It is also given that $\angle 2 \cong \angle 4$. Thus $\angle 3 \cong \angle 4$ by the Transitive Property of Congruence for angles. Hence, by the Corresponding Angles Converse, $p \parallel q$.

PRACTICE   **Can you prove that lines p and q are parallel? Explain why or why not.**

11. $m\angle 1 + m\angle 2 = 180°$

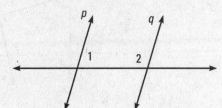

12.

13.

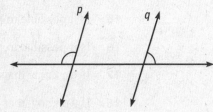

BENCHMARK 2
(Chapters 3 and 4)

5. Use Properties of Perpendicular Lines

Vocabulary Two lines are **perpendicular** if they intersect to form a right angle.

EXAMPLE **Prove Theorem 3.11, the Perpendicular Transversal Theorem: If a transversal is perpendicular to one of two parallel lines then it is perpendicular to the other.**

If a line is perpendicular to one of two parallel lines, then it is perpendicular to the other as well.

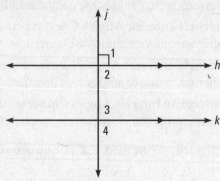

Solution:

Since j is perpendicular to h, they intersect to form four right angles. So both $\angle 1$ and $\angle 2$ are right angles. That is, $m\angle 1 = 90° = m\angle 2$ and we see that $\angle 1 \cong \angle 2$. Since $h \parallel k$, $\angle 1 \cong \angle 3$ and $\angle 2 \cong \angle 4$, by the Corresponding Angles Postulate. Hence $\angle 3 \cong \angle 4$ by the Transitive Property of Congruence for angles. Now $\angle 3$ and $\angle 4$ are a linear pair as well, so that j is perpendicular to k by Theorem 3.8.

PRACTICE **Use the diagram.**

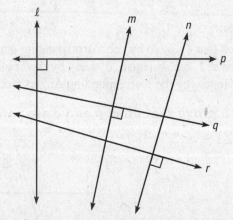

14. Is it possible to prove that a pair of lines are parallel? If so, name them.

15. Is it possible to prove that ℓ is perpendicular to q?

16. Is it possible to prove that n is perpendicular to p?

17. If we know that m is perpendicular to p, which lines are parallel?

18. If we know that $p \parallel r$, which lines are perpendicular?

BENCHMARK 2
(Chapters 3 and 4)

6. Find the Distance from a Point to a Line

Vocabulary

The **distance from a point to a line** is the length of the perpendicular segment from the point to the line. The length of this perpendicular segment is the shortest distance from the point to the line. The **distance between two parallel lines** is the length of any perpendicular segment joining the two lines.

EXAMPLE

What is the distance between the two parallel lines shown in the diagram? Units are in feet.

For every point not on a line, there is a point on the line closest to it. The distance between these points is the distance from the line to the point.

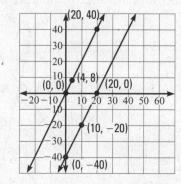

Solution:

You need to find the length of a perpendicular segment from one line to the other. Using the points $(0, -40)$ and $(20, 0)$, the slope of each line is 2, so the slope of a segment perpendicular to each line is $-\frac{1}{2}$. The segment from $(4, 8)$ to $(20, 0)$ has slope $-\frac{1}{2}$. So the distance is $d = \sqrt{(20 - 4)^2 + (0 - 8)^2} \approx 17.9$. The distance between the two lines is about 17.9 feet.

PRACTICE

Use the graph for Exercises 19 and 20.

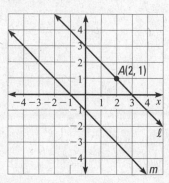

19. What is the distance from point A to line m?

20. What is the distance from line m to line ℓ?

21. Graph the line $y = -2x + 4$. Which point on the line is the shortest distance from the point $(-1, 1)$? What is this distance? Round to the nearest tenth.

22. Graph the line $y = \frac{1}{3}x$. Which point on the line is the shortest distance from the point $(4, -2)$? What is this distance? Round to the nearest tenth.

BENCHMARK 2
(Chapters 3 and 4)

Quiz

1. Draw three lines in space so that two are parallel and each is skew to the third.

2. Draw two parallel lines cut by a transversal and label one pair of same side interior angles 1 and 2, the other pair 3 and 4.

3. Consult your drawing for the previous question and suppose that $m\angle 1 = 37°$. What must be the measures of $\angle 2$, $\angle 3$, and $\angle 4$? Explain.

4. Can you prove that lines p and q are parallel? Explain why or why not.

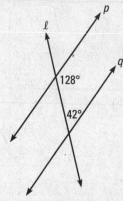

5. What is the distance between the parallel lines $y = 5x + 1$ and $y = 5x - 1$? Round your answer to the nearest hundredth.

BENCHMARK 2
(Chapters 3 and 4)

B. Equations of Lines

When two lines intersect in the coordinate plane, the steeper line has the slope with the greater absolute value. Lines with positive slope slant up to the right, while lines with negative slope slant up to the left. Horizontal lines have slope zero and vertical lines are of undefined slope.

1. Find Slopes of Lines

Vocabulary

The **slope** of the line passing through the points (x_1, y_1) and (x_2, y_2) is given by the formula $m = \dfrac{y_2 - y_1}{x_2 - x_1}$.

EXAMPLE **Find the slope of line *a* and line *d*.**

Slope is the ratio of the "rise" to the "run."

Solution:

Slope of line *a*: $m = \dfrac{y_2 - y_1}{x_2 - x_1} = \dfrac{-1 - (-3)}{-2 - (-4)} = \dfrac{2}{2} = 1$.

Slope of line *d*: $m = \dfrac{y_2 - y_1}{x_2 - x_1} = \dfrac{0 - (-3)}{-4 - (-4)} = \dfrac{3}{0}$, which is undefined.

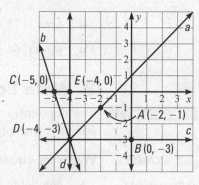

PRACTICE **Use the graph above to find the slope of the given line.**

1. Line *b*
2. Line *c*
3. $\overleftrightarrow{AB}$
4. $\overleftrightarrow{AC}$
5. The *x*-axis
6. The *y*-axis

2. Classify Lines

Vocabulary

Two non-vertical lines in the coordinate plane are **parallel** if and only if they have the same slope. Two non-vertical lines in the coordinate plane are **perpendicular** if and only if the product of their slopes is -1.

EXAMPLE **Find the slope of each line. Which lines are parallel? Which lines are perpendicular?**

All vertical lines are perpendicular to all horizontal lines.

Solution:

Find the slope of line k_1 through

$(-2, 0)$ and $(-4, 2)$: $m_1 = \dfrac{2 - 0}{-4 - (-2)} = \dfrac{2}{-2} = -1$.

Find the slope of line k_2 through

$(-1, 2)$ and $(0, 0)$: $m_2 = \dfrac{0 - 2}{0 - (-1)} = \dfrac{-2}{1} = -2$.

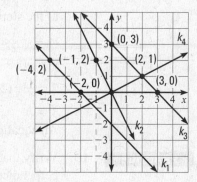

BENCHMARK 2
(Chapters 3 and 4)

Find the slope of line k_3 through $(3, 0)$ and $(0, 3)$: $m_3 = \dfrac{0 - 3}{3 - 0} = \dfrac{-3}{3} = -1$.

Find the slope of line k_4 through $(2, 1)$ and $(0, 0)$: $m_4 = \dfrac{0 - 1}{0 - 2} = \dfrac{-1}{-2} = \dfrac{1}{2}$.

Since $m_1 = m_3$, and these are the only slopes that are equal to each other, k_1 and k_3 is the only pair of parallel lines. Since $m_2 \cdot m_4 = -1$, and these are the only slopes with product -1, $k_2 \perp k_4$ and this is the only pair of perpendicular lines.

PRACTICE **Tell whether the lines through the given points are parallel, perpendicular, or neither. Justify your answer.**

   7. Line 1: $(-4, -5), (2, -1)$ Line 2: $(2, -5), (-2, 1)$

   8. Line 1: $(3, 7), (-1, 4)$ Line 2: $(8, 5), (14, 10)$

   9. Line 1: $(-6, 6), (-2, 10)$ Line 2: $(-8, 9), (-4, 5)$

3. Write Equations of Parallel and Perpendicular Lines

Vocabulary The **slope-intercept form** of a linear equation is $y = mx + b$, where m is the slope and b is the y-intercept.

EXAMPLE **Write an equation of the line passing through the point (2, 2) that is:**

Horizontal lines have equations of the form $y = k$. Vertical lines have equations of the form $x = k$.

   a. parallel to the line $y = 2x + 1$ **b.** perpendicular to the line $y = 2x + 1$

Solution:

   a. The slope m of a line parallel to $y = 2x + 1$ is the same as the slope of this line, so $m = 2$. We find the y-intercept, b, using $m = 2$ and the point $(2, 2)$:

$$y = mx + b$$
$$2 = 2(2) + b$$
$$-2 = b$$

An equation for the line is $y = 2x - 2$.

   b. The slope m of a line perpendicular to $y = 2x + 1$ is the negative reciprocal of the slope of this line, so $m = -\dfrac{1}{2}$. We find the y-intercept, b, using $m = -\dfrac{1}{2}$ and the point $(2, 2)$:

$$y = mx + b$$
$$2 = -\frac{1}{2}(2) + b$$
$$3 = b$$

An equation for the line is $y = -\dfrac{1}{2}x + 3$.

PRACTICE **10.** Verify that the lines found in the example above are actually parallel and perpendicular to the given line by graphing all three on the same set of axes.

   11. Write an equation for the line that passes through $(5, -2)$ and $(2, 1)$.

   12. Write an equation for the line which passes through the point $(0, 0)$ and which is a) parallel to $y = 2x + 8$ and b) perpendicular to $y = -3x - 7$.

BENCHMARK 2
(Chapters 3 and 4)

4. Graph a Line

Vocabulary

The **standard form** of a linear equation is $Ax + By = C$, where A and B are not both zero.

EXAMPLE

Graph $2x + 4y = 8$.

Solution:

Two points determine a line.

The equation is in standard form, so use intercepts.

To find the x-intercept, let $y = 0$. To find the y-intercept, let $x = 0$.

$$2x + 4y = 8 \qquad\qquad 2x + 4y = 8$$

$$2x + 4(0) = 8 \qquad\qquad 2(0) + 4y = 8$$

$$x = 4 \qquad\qquad\qquad y = 2$$

Graph the points $(4, 0)$ and $(0, 2)$ and draw a line through them.

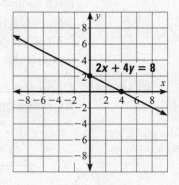

PRACTICE

Graph the equation.

13. $2x + 3y = 12$ **14.** $-5x + 2y = 10$ **15.** $8x - 3y = -12$

Quiz

Refer to the points $A(0, 0)$, $B(2, 2)$, $C(4, 0)$, and $D(2, -1)$.

1. Find an equation for $\overleftrightarrow{AB}$.

2. Find an equation for $\overleftrightarrow{BC}$.

3. Is $\overleftrightarrow{AB} \perp \overleftrightarrow{BC}$?

4. Find an equation of the line through D which is perpendicular to $\overleftrightarrow{BC}$.

5. Find an equation of the line through D which is parallel to $\overleftrightarrow{BC}$.

6. Find the x- and y-intercepts of $\overleftrightarrow{CD}$.

7. Is $\overleftrightarrow{CD} \parallel \overleftrightarrow{AB}$?

BENCHMARK 2
(Chapters 3 and 4)

C. Triangles

A triangle is a polygon with three sides. A triangle with vertices *A*, *B*, and *C* is called "triangle *ABC*" or △*ABC*. We classify angles by their measure. Here we classify triangles by the measure of their angles and the lengths of their sides.

1. Classify Triangles by Sides and Angles

Vocabulary

A **scalene triangle** is a triangle with no congruent sides. An **isosceles triangle** is a triangle with at least two congruent sides. An **equilateral triangle** is a triangle with three congruent sides.

An **acute triangle** is a triangle with three acute angles. A **right triangle** is a triangle with one right angle. An **obtuse triangle** is a triangle with one obtuse angle. An **equiangular triangle** is a triangle with three congruent angles.

EXAMPLE

Copy the triangle and measure its angles. Classify the triangle by its sides and by its angles.

The prefix "iso" means "equal."

a.

b.
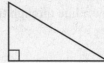

c.
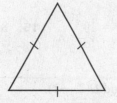

Solution:

a. The triangle has a pair of congruent sides so it is isosceles. We measure the angles as 25°, 25°, and 130° so it is an obtuse isosceles triangle.

b. The triangle has angles of measure 30°, 60°, and 90° and no congruent sides. It is a scalene right triangle.

c. All three sides are congruent so the triangle is isosceles and also equilateral. The measure of each angle is 60°, so it is an acute, equiangular, isosceles, equilateral triangle.

PRACTICE **If possible, draw a triangle that fits each description.**

1. A scalene acute triangle.

2. An obtuse right triangle.

3. An acute isosceles triangle which is not equiangular.

4. A right isosceles triangle.

BENCHMARK 2
C. Triangles

BENCHMARK 2
(Chapters 3 and 4)

2. Use the Triangle Sum Theorem

Theorem The **Triangle Sum Theorem** states that the sum of the measures of the interior angles of a triangle is 180°.

EXAMPLE **Find the measure of each angle in the triangle below.**

Are you convinced that the measures of the angles of a triangle always sum to 180°?

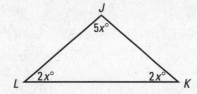

Solution:

Set up an equation to solve for x.

$m\angle J + m\angle K + m\angle L = 180°$	**Triangle Sum Theorem**
$5x° + 2x° + 2x° = 180°$	**Substitution**
$9x° = 180°$	**Collect like terms.**
$x = 20$	**Divide both sides by 9°.**

Thus, $m\angle J = 5(20)° = 100°$, $m\angle K = 2(20)° = 40°$ and $m\angle L = 2(20)° = 40°$.

PRACTICE **Find the measure of each angle in the triangle shown.**

5.

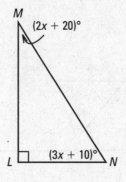

6.

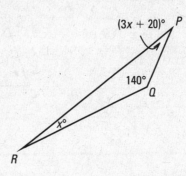

7.

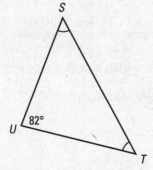

BENCHMARK 2
C. Triangles

BENCHMARK 2
(Chapters 3 and 4)

3. Use the Third Angles Theorem

Theorem The **Third Angles Theorem** states that if two angles of one triangle are congruent to two angles of another triangle, then the third angles are also congruent.

EXAMPLE Use the third angles theorem to find $m\angle BCD$.

Always figure out the missing angles in a diagram if you can.

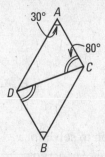

Solution:

$\angle A \cong \angle B$ and $\angle ACD \cong \angle BDC$, so by the Third Angles Theorem,

$\angle BCD \cong \angle ADC$. By the Triangle Sum Theorem,

$m\angle ADC = 180° - 80° - 30° = 70°$.

So, $m\angle BCD = m\angle ADC = 70°$ by the definition of congruent angles.

PRACTICE Use the diagram to answer the questions.

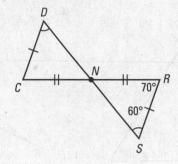

8. In the diagram, what is $m\angle DCN$?

9. By the definition of congruence, what additional information is needed to know that $\triangle NDC \cong \triangle NSR$?

10. If you know that $\triangle NDC \cong \triangle NSR$, which side is congruent to $\overline{DN}$?

11. What must be the measure of angles $\angle SNR$ and $\angle DNC$?

BENCHMARK 2
(Chapters 3 and 4)

4. Apply the Base Angles Theorem

Vocabulary Given an isosceles triangle, the **legs** are the two congruent sides. The **vertex angle** is the angle formed by the legs. The **base** is the third side. The **base angles** are the angles adjacent to the base.

EXAMPLE **a.** In $\triangle DEF$, $\overline{DE} \cong \overline{DF}$. Name two congruent angles and find their measures.

b. Find the values of x and y in the diagram.

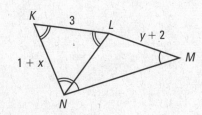

Solution:

a. $\overline{DE} \cong \overline{DF}$, so by the Base Angles Theorem, $\angle E \cong \angle F$. By the Angle Sum Theorem, $m\angle E = 180° - 20° - m\angle F = 160° - m\angle E$, since $m\angle E = m\angle F$ by the definition of congruent angles. Thus, $m\angle E = 80° = m\angle F$.

b. Find the value of x. Because $\triangle KLN$ is equiangular, it is also equilateral and $\overline{KN} \cong \overline{KL}$. Therefore, $1 + x = 3$ and $x = 2$.

Next, find the value of y. Because $\angle LNM \cong \angle LMN$, $\overline{LN} \cong \overline{LM}$ and $\triangle LMN$ is isosceles. We also know that $LN = 3$ because $\triangle KLN$ is equilateral. Thus, $LN = LM$ so that $3 = y + 2$ and $y = 1$.

> Base angles of an isosceles triangle have sides of the same length and intercept sides of the same length, so they *must* have the same measure.

PRACTICE **Find the values of x and y.**

12.

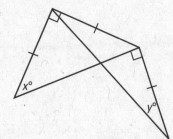

13.

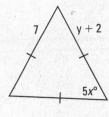

14.

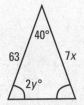

15.

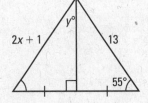

BENCHMARK 2
C. Triangles

BENCHMARK 2
(Chapters 3 and 4)

Quiz

1. If the perimeter of an equilateral triangle is 33, what is the length of any of the three sides?

2. If two sides of a triangle have length 8 and the angle that they form has measure 28°, what are the measures of the remaining angles?

3. Are acute triangles ever right triangles? Explain.

4. A base angle in an isosceles triangle measures 80°. Find the measure of the vertex angle.

5. If the area of an isosceles right triangle is 32, what is the length of each leg?

**BENCHMARK 2
C. Triangles**

BENCHMARK 2
(Chapters 3 and 4)

D. Proving Triangles are Congruent

Often in mathematics, we are required to make a determination based on an incomplete set of facts. Sometimes our problem has certain characteristics which are very similar to another situation about which we know a great deal. Knowing when the results from the familiar setting carry over into our own is very important. In geometry, if we can show two figures are congruent, then we can extend what is known about one figure to the other.

1. Show that Figures are Congruent

Vocabulary

Congruent figures have exactly the same size and shape. In particular, two polygons are congruent if all corresponding sides and angles are congruent.

EXAMPLE

Two figures are congruent if you could trace one from the other.

If you divide a rectangular wall into pink and blue sections along the path _EFGH_, as shown in the diagram, will the sections of the wall be the same size and shape?

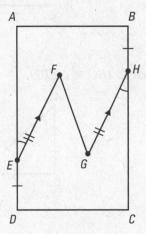

Solution:

Since it is given that _ABCD_ is a rectangle, $\overline{AB} \cong \overline{CD}$. Since $AD = BC$ and the diagram shows that $\overline{DE} \cong \overline{BH}$, we must have that $\overline{AE} \cong \overline{CH}$. $\overline{EF} \cong \overline{HG}$ is given and $\overline{FG} \cong \overline{FG}$ since congruence of segments is reflexive. Thus all the corresponding sides are congruent. Also, since _ABCD_ is a rectangle, all of its angles are right angles. In particular, $\angle A \cong \angle C$ and $\angle B \cong \angle D$. Further, we are given that $\angle AEF \cong \angle CHG$. This implies that $\angle DEF$ and $\angle BHG$ are congruent since they form linear pairs with $\angle AEF$ and $\angle CHG$ respectively. It remains only to be shown that $\angle EFG \cong \angle HGF$. This is true since the diagram shows that $\overline{EF} \parallel \overline{HG}$ and these line segments are cut by the transversal $\overline{FG}$ so that $\angle AEF \cong \angle CHG$ by the Alternating Interior Angles Theorem. So all the corresponding angles are congruent and we can say that $ABHGFE \cong CDEFGH$.

BENCHMARK 2
(Chapters 3 and 4)

PRACTICE

1. Find the values of x, y, and z so that $ABCD \cong EFGH$.

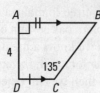 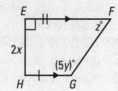

2. The figures below are congruent and we can write $QXYZT \cong$ _____.

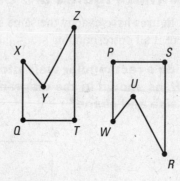

3. Prove that $\triangle ABC \cong \triangle EBD$.

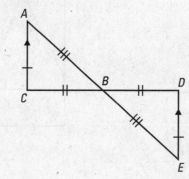

4. If $\triangle GHI \cong \triangle GHJ$, what can be said about the relationship between the ray $\overrightarrow{HG}$ and the angle $\angle IHJ$?

2. Use the SSS Congruence Postulate

Postulate

The **Side-Side-Side (SSS) Congruence Postulate** states that if three sides of one triangle are congruent to three sides of another triangle, then the two triangles are congruent.

EXAMPLE

Given that $\overline{PQ} \cong \overline{SR}$ and $\overline{PR} \cong \overline{SQ}$, write a proof showing that $\triangle PRQ \cong \triangle SQR$.

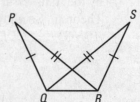

Convince yourself of the SSS Congruence Postulate.

Solution:

Proof: It is given that $\overline{PQ} \cong \overline{SR}$ and $\overline{PR} \cong \overline{SQ}$. By the Reflexive Property, $\overline{QR} \cong \overline{QR}$. So, by the SSS Congruence Postulate, $\triangle PRQ \cong \triangle SQR$.

BENCHMARK 2
(Chapters 3 and 4)

PRACTICE   **Decide whether the congruence statement is true. Explain your reasoning.**

5. $\triangle DFG \cong \triangle HJK$

 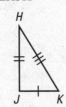

6. $\triangle ABC \cong \triangle CDA$

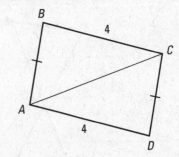

7. $\triangle HIJ \cong \triangle KLM$

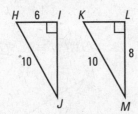

8. $\triangle ABC \cong \triangle DEF$

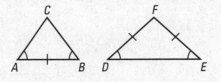

3. Use the SAS Congruence Postulate

Postulate   The **Side-Angle-Side (SAS) Congruence Postulate** states that if two sides and the included angle of one triangle are congruent to two sides and the included angle of another triangle, then the two triangles are congruent.

EXAMPLE   **Given that $\overline{EH} \cong \overline{FG}$ and $\overline{EH} \parallel \overline{FG}$, prove that $\triangle EHF \cong \triangle GFH$.**

Do you believe the SAS Congruence Postulate?

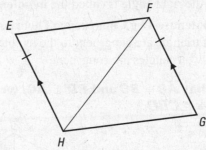

Solution:

Statements	Reasons
S **1.** $\overline{EH} \cong \overline{FG}$	**1.** Given
2. $\overline{EH} \parallel \overline{FG}$	**2.** Given
A **3.** $\angle FHE \cong \angle HFG$	**3.** Alternate Interior Angles Theorem
S **4.** $\overline{HF} \cong \overline{FH}$	**4.** Reflexive Property of Congruence
5. $\triangle EHF \cong \triangle GFH$	**5.** SAS Congruence Postulate

BENCHMARK 2
(Chapters 3 and 4)

PRACTICE **Decide whether enough information is given to prove that the triangles are congruent using the SAS Congruence Postulate.**

9. $\triangle ABC \cong \triangle EDC$

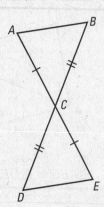

10. $\triangle PQS \cong \triangle SQR$

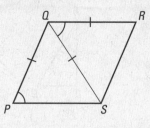

11. $\triangle GHI \cong \triangle JLK$

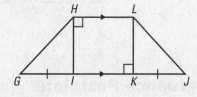

12. $\triangle MPN \cong \triangle NQO$

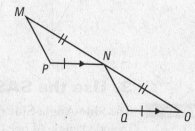

4. Use the Hypotenuse-Leg Congruence Theorem

Vocabulary In a right triangle, the sides adjacent to the right angles are called **legs**. The side opposite the right angle is called the **hypotenuse** of the right triangle.

Theorem The **Hypotenuse-Leg Congruence Theorem** states that if the hypotenuse and a leg of a right triangle are congruent to the hypotenuse and a leg of a second right triangle, then the two triangles are congruent.

EXAMPLE **Given that $\overline{AB} \cong \overline{BC}$ and $\overline{BD} \perp \overline{AC}$, write a proof showing that $\triangle ABD \cong \triangle CBD$.**

The hypotenuse is always the longest side of a right triangle.

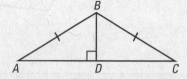

Solution:

You may wish to redraw the triangles side by side so that corresponding parts are in the same position.

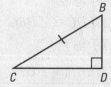

BENCHMARK 2
(Chapters 3 and 4)

Statements	Reasons
H 1. $\overline{AB} \cong \overline{BC}$	**1.** Given
2. $\overline{BD} \perp \overline{AD}; \overline{BD} \perp \overline{CD}$	**2.** Given
3. $\angle ADB$ and $\angle CDB$ are right angles	**3.** Definition of $\perp$ lines
4. $\triangle ABD$ and $\triangle CBD$ are right triangles	**4.** Definition of right triangle
L 5. $\overline{BD} \cong \overline{BD}$	**5.** Reflexive property of congruence
6. $\triangle ABD \cong \triangle CBD$	**6.** HL Congruence Theorem

PRACTICE   Quadrilateral **ABCD** is a rectangle in the figure.

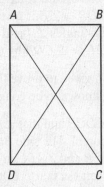
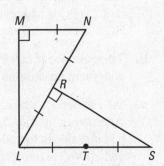

13. Redraw $\triangle ABD$ and $\triangle CDB$ with corresponding parts in the same position.

14. Use the Hypotenuse-Leg Theorem to prove that $\triangle ABD \cong \triangle CDB$.

15. Redraw $\triangle MNL$ and $\triangle RLS$ with corresponding parts in the same position.

16. Use the Hypotenuse-Leg Theorem to prove that $\triangle MNL \cong \triangle RLS$.

5. Use ASA and AAS Congruence

Postulate   The **Angle-Side-Angle (ASA) Congruence Postulate** states that if two angles and the included side of one triangle are congruent to two angles and the included side of another triangle, then the two triangles are congruent.

Theorem   The **Angle-Angle-Side (AAS) Congruence Theorem** states that if two angles and a non-included side of one triangle are congruent to two angles and a non-included side of another triangle, then the two triangles are congruent.

BENCHMARK 2
(Chapters 3 and 4)

EXAMPLE   **Can the triangles be proven congruent with the information given in the diagram? If so, state the postulate or theorem you would use.**

WARNING:
There is no
AAA Congruence
Theorem or
Postulate.

a.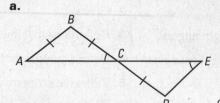

b. **c.**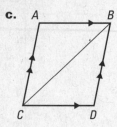

Solution:

a. The vertical angles $\angle ACB$ and $\angle DCE$ are congruent to each other. They are also congruent to $\angle E$, since $\angle ACB \cong \angle E$ is given, and to $\angle A$, since it is given that $\triangle ABC$ is isosceles with base angles $\angle A$ and $\angle C$. Since we are given that $\overline{BC} \cong \overline{CD}$, we can say that $\triangle ABC \cong \triangle CDE$ by the AAS Congruence Postulate.

b. There is not enough information given to prove that these triangles are congruent because no sides are known to be congruent.

c. We can deduce that $\angle ABC \cong \angle DCB$ and that $\angle ACB \cong \angle DBC$ by the Alternating Interior Angles Theorem. The side $\overline{BC}$ is congruent to itself, and this side is included by $\angle ACB$ and $\angle ABC$ in one triangle and by $\angle DCB$ and $\angle DBC$ in the other. So we can say that $\triangle BAC \cong \triangle CDB$ by the ASA Congruence Postulate.

PRACTICE   **17.** Name a pair of congruent triangles. Which postulate or theorem would you use to prove the pair are congruent?

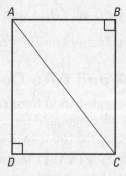

18. For which values of x will the ASA Postulate apply to show that $\triangle ABC \cong \triangle DEF$?

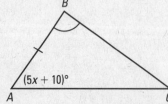 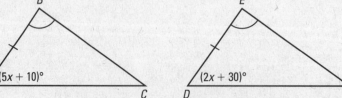

BENCHMARK 2
(Chapters 3 and 4)

19. For which values of x will the AAS Congruence Theorem apply to show that $\triangle PQR \cong \triangle TUV$?

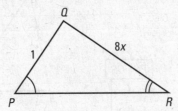 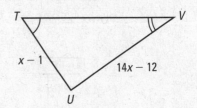

20. Is it possible to conclude from the diagram that the triangles are congruent? If so, by which postulate or theorem?

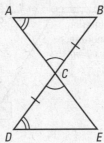

6. Write a Flow Proof

Vocabulary A **flow proof** uses arrows to show the flow of a logical argument. Each reason is written below the statement it justifies.

EXAMPLE **In the diagram, $\overline{CE} \perp \overline{BD}$ and $\triangle CAB \cong \triangle CAD$. Write a flow proof to show that $\triangle ABE \cong \triangle ADE$.**

Writing a flow proof helps to organize your thoughts.

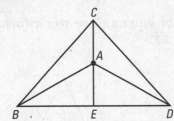

Solution:

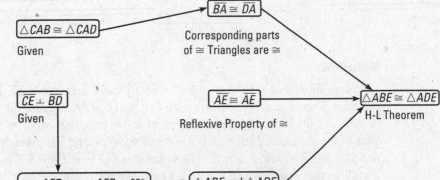

BENCHMARK 2
(Chapters 3 and 4)

PRACTICE   **21.** Copy and complete the following flow proof.

Given: $\overline{PQ} \parallel \overline{RS}$ and $\overline{PS} \parallel \overline{QR}$

Prove: $\triangle PRS \cong \triangle RPQ$

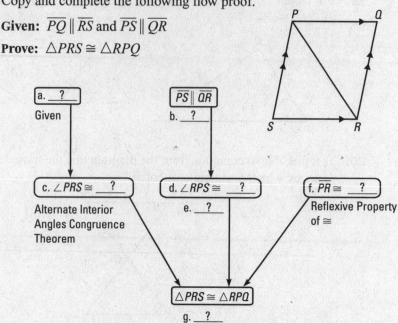

7. Use Congruent Triangles

Vocabulary   If $\triangle ABC \cong \triangle XYZ$ then A **corresponds** to X, B corresponds to Y, and C corresponds to Z. The angles and sides determined by these vertices are correspondingly congruent. That is, **corresponding parts** of congruent triangles are congruent.

EXAMPLE   **Explain how you can use the information given in the diagram to show that $\overline{PQ} \cong \overline{ST}$.**

Sometimes it helps to redraw a diagram using a different orientation when proving two figures are congruent.

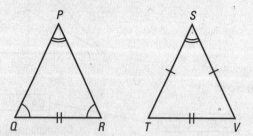

Solution:

If we can show that $\triangle PQR \cong \triangle STV$ we will know that $\overline{PQ} \cong \overline{ST}$. First, copy the diagram. Then add all the information that you can deduce. In this case, since $\triangle STV$ is isosceles, its base angles are congruent so we have that $m\angle T = m\angle V$. Since the sum of the angles in a triangle is $180°$ and $m\angle P = m\angle S$ is given, it follows that $m\angle Q + m\angle R = m\angle T + m\angle V$. Now since $m\angle Q = m\angle R$ it follows that $2m\angle Q = 2m\angle T$ so that $m\angle Q = m\angle T$ and $\angle Q \cong T$. We are given $\angle P \cong \angle S$ and $\overline{QR} \cong \overline{TV}$ so by the AAS Congruence Theorem, $\triangle PQR \cong \triangle STV$ and $\overline{PQ} \cong \overline{ST}$.

BENCHMARK 2
(Chapters 3 and 4)

PRACTICE   Tell which triangles you can show are congruent in order to prove the statement. Which postulate or theorem would you use?

22. $\angle CBD \cong \angle EDB$

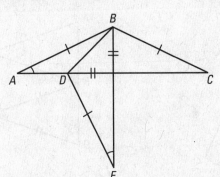

23. $\angle DAB \cong \angle DBA$

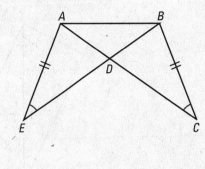

24. $\overline{LO} \cong \overline{NO}$

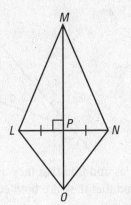

25. $\overline{XZ} \cong \overline{YW}$

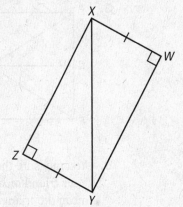

BENCHMARK 2
(Chapters 3 and 4)

Quiz

In Exercises 1–4, identify a pair of congruent triangles in the figure. Justify your answer.

1.

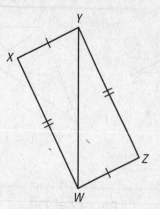

2.

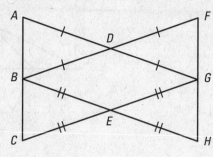

3.

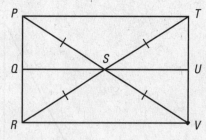

4.

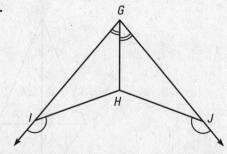

5. You measure the angles of two triangles and find that they are both equiangular. Your friend measures the sides and find that they are both equilateral. Does this mean the triangles are congruent? Explain.

6. You measure the angles of two other triangles and find them to be right triangles. Your friend measures their side lengths and finds the hypotenuse of each to be 9 inches long. Now must the triangles be congruent? Explain.

BENCHMARK 2
(Chapters 3 and 4)

E. Congruence Transformations

1. Rigid Motions and Congruence

Vocabulary   A **rigid motion** is a transformation that preserves length and angle measure.

EXAMPLE   **Are the two figures shown congruent?**

Solution:

Two figures are congruent if there is a series of rigid
motions that can move one figure onto the other.
If the top triangle is reflected over the *x*-axis, it will
be moved onto the bottom triangle. Therefore,
the two triangles are congruent.

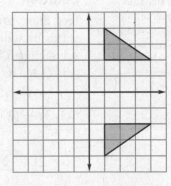

PRACTICE   **Describe the transformation(s) you can use, if any, to move one figure onto the other. Then state if the two figures are congruent.**

1.
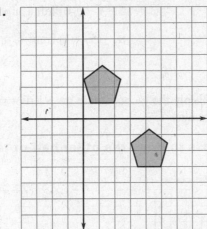

2.
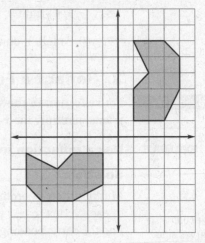

3.
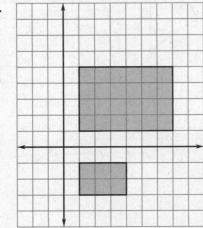

4.
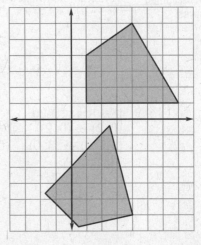

BENCHMARK 2
E. Congruence Transformations

BENCHMARK 2
(Chapters 3 and 4)

2. Translate a Figure

Vocabulary

A **translation** is a transformation that moves every point of an object the same distance in the same direction.

EXAMPLE

Figure **ABCD** has the vertices **A**(−2, 5), **B**(0, 6), **C**(1, 3), and **D**(−1, 3). Sketch **ABCD** and its image after the translation (**x**, **y**) → (**x** + 2, **y** − 5).

A translation preserves side lengths and angle measures.

Solution:

First draw *ABCD*. Find the translation of each vertex by adding 2 to its *x*-coordinate and subtracting 5 from its *y*-coordinate. Then draw *ABCD* and its image. $(x, y) \rightarrow (x + 2, y - 5)$

$A(-2, 5) \rightarrow (0, 0)$ $B(0, 6) \rightarrow (2, 1)$
$C(1, 3) \rightarrow (3, -2)$ $D(-1, 3) \rightarrow (1, -2)$

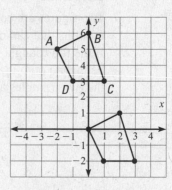

PRACTICE

Give the new coordinates of the given point after the described translation.

5. (−3, 4) right 1, down 3

6. (−2, 0) left 1, up 3

7. (0, 3) left 3, down 6

8. (5, −1) right 4, up 3

3. Reflect a Figure

Vocabulary

For **reflection in the x-axis**, multiply the *y*-coordinate by −1. For **reflection in the y-axis**, multiply the *x*-coordinate by −1.

EXAMPLE

Use a reflection in the *y*-axis to draw the other half of the figure.

Solution:

A reflection also preserves side length and angle measures.

Multiply the *x*-coordinate of each vertex by −1 to find the corresponding vertex in the image.

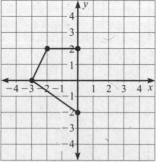
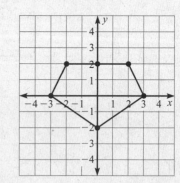

$(x, y) \rightarrow (-x, y)$
$(0, 2) \rightarrow (0, 2)$ $(-2, 2) \rightarrow (2, 2)$
$(-3, 0) \rightarrow (3, 0)$ $(0, -2) \rightarrow (0, -2)$

BENCHMARK 2
E. Congruence Transformations

BENCHMARK 2
(Chapters 3 and 4)

PRACTICE   **Give the new coordinates of the given point after the described reflection.**

9. $(-3, 4)$ in the x-axis   **10.** $(-2, 0)$ in the y-axis

11. $(0, 3)$ in the y-axis   **12.** $(5, -1)$ in the x-axis

4. Identify Rotations

Vocabulary   In a rotation, the **angle of rotation** is formed by rays drawn from the center of rotation through corresponding points on the original figure and its image.

EXAMPLE

Rotations preserve side length and angle measures.

Graph $\overline{AB}$ and $\overline{CD}$. Tell whether $\overline{CD}$ is a rotation of $\overline{AB}$ about the origin. If so, give the angle and direction of rotation.

a. $A(1, 1), B(4, 1), C(-1, 1), D(-1, 4)$

b. $A(2, 0), B(5, 0), C(-2, 0), D(0, 5)$

Solution:

a. $m\angle AOC = m\angle BOD = 90°$.

This is a 90° counterclockwise rotation.

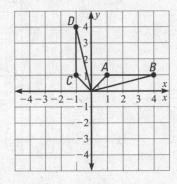

b. $m\angle AOC = 180°$ but $m\angle BOD = 90°$.

This is not a rotation.

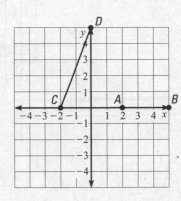

PRACTICE   **Give the new coordinates of the given point after the described rotation.**

13. $(-3, 4)$ clockwise 90°   **14.** $(-2, 0)$ counterclockwise 180°

15. $(0, 3)$ clockwise 270°   **16.** $(5, -1)$ counterclockwise 90°

BENCHMARK 2
E. Congruence Transformations

BENCHMARK 2
(Chapters 3 and 4)

Quiz

Each figure shows a transformation of the labeled polygon. Describe the transformation in each case.

1. Explain why the figures in Section 1 are congruent.

2.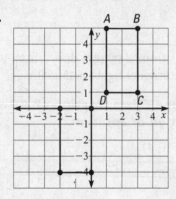

3.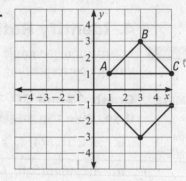

4.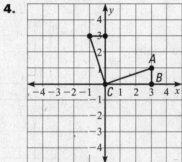

5.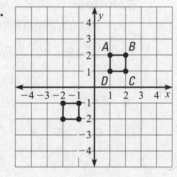

6.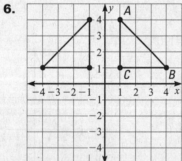

7.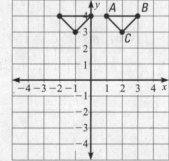

BENCHMARK 3
(Chapters 5, 6, and 7)

A. Special Segments in Triangles

A triangle consists of three line segments. There are other segments related to triangles. Their positions relative to each other provides us with additional information.

1. Use the Midsegment Theorem

Vocabulary A **midsegment** of a triangle connects the midpoints of two sides of a triangle. Every triangle has three midsegments.

Theorem The **Midsegment Theorem** states that the segment connecting the midpoints of two sides of a triangle is parallel to the third side and is half as long as that side.

EXAMPLE In the diagram, $\overline{AB}$ and $\overline{BC}$ are midsegments of $\triangle DEF$. Find BC and DE.

Midsegments are parallel to the side of the triangle that they do not touch.

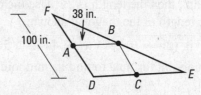

Solution:

$BC = \dfrac{1}{2} \cdot DF = \dfrac{1}{2}(100 \text{ in.}) = 50 \text{ in.}$

$DE = 2 \cdot AB = 2(38 \text{ in.}) = 76 \text{ in.}$

PRACTICE The figure shows $\triangle ABC$ and the midpoints of all its sides. Use it to find the length of the segment.

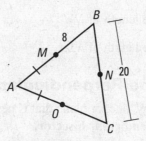

1. $\overline{OM}$ _____

2. $\overline{AB}$ _____

3. $\overline{ON}$ _____

4. $\overline{AO}$ _____

5. $\overline{AC}$ _____

6. $\overline{MN}$ _____

**BENCHMARK 3
A. Segments in Triangles**

BENCHMARK 3
(Chapters 5, 6, and 7)

2. Place a Figure in a Coordinate Plane

Vocabulary

A **coordinate proof** involves placing a geometric figure in a coordinate plane.

EXAMPLE

Place a rectangle whose width is half its length in the coordinate plane. Use the coordinates to find the length of a diagonal and that diagonal's midpoint.

It is convenient to use (0, 0) as an endpoint when placing figures in the plane.

Solution:

Since it is easy to find lengths of horizontal and vertical segments and distances from (0, 0), place one vertex at the origin and one or more sides on an axis. If we let w stand for the width, then the length is $2w$. Use the distance formula to find the length of the diagonal shown:

$$\sqrt{(w - 0)^2 + (2w - 0)^2} = \sqrt{w^2 + 4w^2} = \sqrt{5w^2} = w\sqrt{5}.$$

Use the midpoint formula to find its midpoint:

$$\left(\frac{0 + w}{2}, \frac{0 + 2w}{2}\right) = \left(\frac{w}{2}, w\right).$$

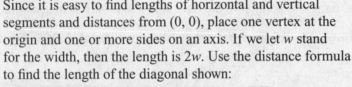

PRACTICE

Use the figure from the example above.

7. Find the coordinates of the midpoint, N, of $\overline{AB}$.

8. Find the coordinates of the midpoint, L, of $\overline{BC}$.

9. Find the length of LM.

10. Find the length of NM.

11. Find the length of NL.

3. Use the Perpendicular Bisector Theorem

Vocabulary

A segment, ray, line, or plane that is perpendicular to a segment at its midpoint is called a **perpendicular bisector**.

Theorem

The **Perpendicular Bisector Theorem** states that in a plane, if a point is equidistant from the endpoints of a segment, then it is on the perpendicular bisector of the segment.

EXAMPLE

In the diagram, $\overleftrightarrow{EB}$ is the perpendicular bisector of $\overline{CD}$.

WARNING:

A segment bisector is not always a perpendicular bisector.

a. Which segment lengths in the diagram are equal?

b. Is A on $\overleftrightarrow{EB}$?

c. Solve for x.

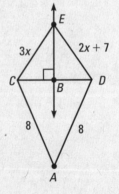

BENCHMARK 3
A. Segments in Triangles

BENCHMARK 3
(Chapters 5, 6, and 7)

Solution:

a. $\overleftrightarrow{EB}$ bisects $\overline{CD}$ so $CB = BD$. Because E is on the perpendicular bisector of $\overline{CD}$, $EC = ED$ by Theorem 5.2. The diagram shows that $CA = DA = 8$.

b. Because $CA = DA$, A is equidistant from C and D. So, by the Converse of the Perpendicular Bisector Theorem, A is on the perpendicular bisector of $\overline{CD}$, which is $\overleftrightarrow{EB}$.

c. $EC = ED$ so that $3x = 2x + 7$. Solve to get $x = 7$.

PRACTICE

In the figure, both **C** and **D** lie on the perpendicular bisector of $\overline{AB}$ and **M** is the midpoint of $\overline{AB}$.

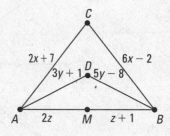

12. List all pairs of congruent segments.

13. Name a pair of obtuse triangles which are congruent and the theorem or postulate that justifies this assertion.

14. Solve for x.   15. Solve for y.   16. Solve for z.

4. Use the Angle Bisector Theorems

Vocabulary

An **angle bisector** is a ray that divides an angle into two congruent adjacent angles. The **distance from a point to a line** is the length of the perpendicular segment from the point to the line.

Theorem

The **Angle Bisector Theorem** states that if a point is on the bisector of an angle, then it is equidistant from the two sides of the angle.

EXAMPLE

Be sure the hypotheses of a theorem are satisfied before applying it.

Find the measure of ∠BAD.

Solution:
Because $\overline{DB} \perp \overrightarrow{AB}$ and $\overline{DC} \perp \overrightarrow{AC}$ and $DB = CD$, $\overrightarrow{AD}$ bisects ∠BAC by the Converse of the Angle Bisector Theorem. So, $m\angle BAD = \frac{1}{2}m\angle BAC = \frac{1}{2}(68°) = 34°$.

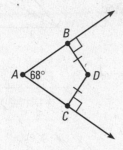

BENCHMARK 3
A. Segments in Triangles

Name _____   Date _____

BENCHMARK 3
(Chapters 5, 6, and 7)

PRACTICE   **Find the value of x.**

17.

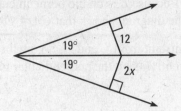

18.

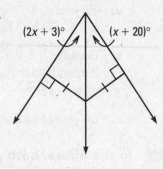

19.

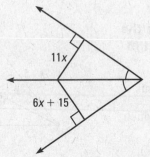

20. Do you have enough information to conclude that $\overrightarrow{QP}$ bisects $\angle SQR$?

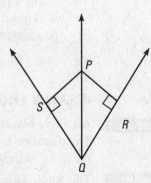

5. Use the Concurrency of Bisectors

Vocabulary   The point of concurrency of the three perpendicular bisectors of a triangle is called the **circumcenter** of the triangle. The point of concurrency of the three angle bisectors of a triangle is called the **incenter** of the triangle.

EXAMPLE

a. Find the coordinates of the circumcenter, G, of the triangle with vertices $A(-3, 0)$, $B(3, 0)$, and $C(2, 3)$.

The circumcenter is the center of a circle that circumscribes the triangle.

b. In the diagram, M is the incenter of $\triangle DEF$. Find MA.

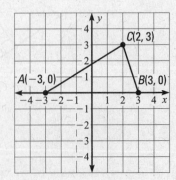

Solution:

a. Draw $\triangle ABC$ in the coordinate plane and observe that G lies on the x-axis since $(0, 0)$ is the midpoint of $\overline{AB}$. So its coordinates are $(0, y)$ for some y. Since $GA = GC$, by the distance formula we have

$$\sqrt{(-3 - 0)^2 + (y - 0)^2} = \sqrt{(2 - 0)^2 + (3 - y)^2}.$$

Squaring both sides and collecting like terms, $6y = 4$ so that $y = \frac{2}{3}$ and the coordinates of G are $\left(0, \frac{2}{3}\right)$.

BENCHMARK 3
(Chapters 5, 6, and 7)

b. By the Concurrency of the Angle Bisectors of a Triangle Theorem, the incenter M is equidistant from the sides of $\triangle DEF$. So, to find MA, you can find MB in $\triangle DEF$. By the Pythagorean Theorem,

$$12^2 = 8^2 + MB^2$$
$$144 = 64 + MB^2$$
$$80 = MB^2$$
$$\sqrt{80} = 4\sqrt{5} = MB.$$

Hence, $MA = MB = 4\sqrt{5}$.

PRACTICE **Use the coordinates given for _A_, _B_, and _C_ to find the coordinates of the circumcenter of $\triangle ABC$.**

21. $A(0, 4)$, $B(0, -4)$, $C(4, 1)$

22. $A(-1, 2)$, $B(2, 3)$, $C(2, -1)$

23. $A(-4, -4)$, $B(0, 0)$, $C(4, -4)$

24. Suppose in part b of the example above you are not given MF or BF, but you are given that $BE = 4$ and $ME = 8$. Find MA.

6. Use the Centroid of a Triangle

Vocabulary A **median of a triangle** is a segment from a vertex to the midpoint of the opposite side.

Theorem The **Concurrency of Medians of a Triangle Theorem** states that the medians of a triangle intersect at a point called the **centroid,** that is two thirds of the distance from each vertex to the midpoint of the opposite side.

EXAMPLE **Find the coordinates of the centroid, _P_, of $\triangle FGH$ where the vertices are _F_(1,1), _G_(3, 6) and _H_(5, 5). Also, if _K_ is the midpoint of $\overline{HF}$, find _GP_, _PK_, and _GK_.**

The centroid is the triangle's center of mass.

Solution:

Sketch $\triangle FGH$. Then use the Midpoint Formula to find the coordinates of K and sketch the median $\overline{GK}$.

$K\left(\dfrac{5+1}{2}, \dfrac{5+1}{2}\right) = K(3, 3)$

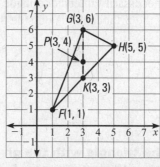

P is two thirds of the distance from each vertex to the midpoint of the opposite side.

The distance from vertex $G(3, 6)$ to $K(3, 3)$ is $6 - 3 = 3$ units. So the centroid is $\dfrac{2}{3}(3) = 2$ units down from G on $\overline{GK}$. So the coordinates of the centroid P are $(3, 4)$. It is easy to see then that $GP = 2$, $PK = 1$, and $GK = 3$.

BENCHMARK 3
A. Segments in Triangles

BENCHMARK 3
(Chapters 5, 6, and 7)

PRACTICE **Find the centroid of the triangle with the given vertices.**

25. $A(2, 5)$, $B(0, -2)$, $C(4, 0)$ **26.** $A(0, 0)$, $B(-3, -1)$, $C(3, -2)$

27. $A(0, 3)$, $B(0, 0)$, $C(3, 6)$ **28.** $A(0, 3)$, $B(-1, 0)$, $C(1, 0)$

7. Find the Orthocenter of a Triangle

Vocabulary An **altitude of a triangle** is the perpendicular segment from a vertex to the opposite side or to the line that contains the opposite side. The point of concurrency of the three altitudes of a triangle is called the **orthocenter** of the triangle.

EXAMPLE **Sketch the three altitudes of each triangle to locate the orthocenter.**

a.   b. 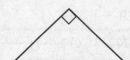   c.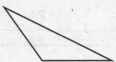

Solution:

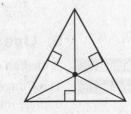

a. This is an equiangular triangle. Notice that each altitude appears to be an angle bisector as well as a median. This is, in fact, the case. So the orthocenter is the same as the incenter, circumcenter, and centroid.

The legs of a right triangle form two of its altitudes.

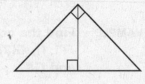

b. This is a right triangle. Notice that two altitudes are actually the legs of the triangle so we know where the orthocenter must be before we even draw the third altitude. The orthocenter must be the vertex of the right angle.

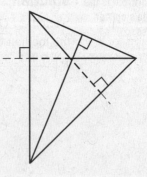

c. Notice that only one altitude has points in the interior of an obtuse triangle so that the other two necessarily intersect outside the triangle. Thus the orthocenter is outside the triangle.

PRACTICE **Sketch the triangle with the given vertices together with its altitudes. Say whether the orthocenter is inside, outside, or on the triangle.**

29. $A(2, 5)$, $B(0, -2)$, $C(4, 0)$ **30.** $A(0, 0)$, $B(-3, -1)$, $C(6, -2)$

31. $A(0, 3)$, $B(0, 0)$, $C(3, 6)$ **32.** $A(0, 3)$, $B(-1, 0)$, $C(1, 0)$

BENCHMARK 3
A. Segments in Triangles

BENCHMARK 3
(Chapters 5, 6, and 7)

Quiz

1. Graph the triangle with vertices $A(0, 10)$, $B(8, 0)$ and $C(0, 0)$ together with its midsegments. Find the length of each midsegment.

2. Find the coordinates of the midpoints, M and N, of the sides $\overline{AB}$ and $\overline{BC}$, respectively, in a triangle with the vertices $A(-a, 0)$, $B(0, b)$, and $C(a, 0)$. Then find the length of the midsegment $\overline{MN}$.

3. Use the figure to find the value of x:

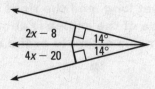

4. Find the coordinates of the orthocenter of the triangle with vertices $G(0, 10)$, $H(10, 0)$, and $I(-10, 0)$.

5. Find the coordinates of the centroid of the triangle whose vertices are $A(5, 2)$, $B(2, -2)$, and $C(5, 12)$.

6. Find the coordinates of the circumcenter of the triangle with vertices $(-4, 0)$, $(4, 0)$, and $(1, 5)$.

BENCHMARK 3
(Chapters 5, 6, and 7)

B. Inequalities in Triangles

Knowing the length of the sides of a triangle gives information about the measures of the angles. Conversely, knowing the measures of the angles of a triangle gives information about the lengths of the sides.

1. Relate Side Length and Angle Measure

EXAMPLE

We can immediately eliminate choice *C* since a triangle with an angle of 22° cannot also have one of 175° since the sum of the angle measures is 180° in any triangle.

You are constructing a stage prop of a large triangular mountain. The bottom edge of the mountain is about 57 feet long. The left slope is about 22 feet long, and the right slope is about 40 feet long. You are told that one of the angles is about 22° and one is about 13°. Find the most reasonable estimate of the measure of the peak of the mountain.

A. 120°   **B.** 145°   **C.** 175°   **D.** 90°

Solution:

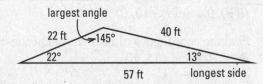

Draw a diagram and label the side lengths. The peak angle is opposite the longest side given so, by Theorem 5.10, the peak angle is the largest angle. The angle measures sum to 180°, so the third angle measure is 180° − (22° + 13°) = 145°. You can now label the angle measures in your diagram. The greatest angle measure is 145° so this is the measure of the peak angle and the correct answer is B.

PRACTICE   List the sides or angles in order from smallest to largest.

1.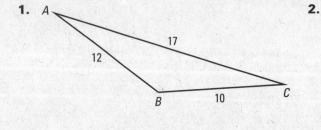

2.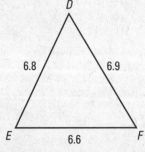

3.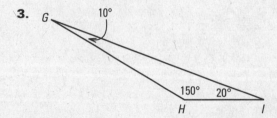

4.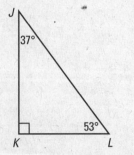

BENCHMARK 3
(Chapters 5, 6, and 7)

5.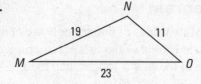

6.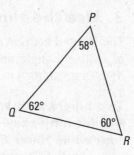

2. Use the Triangle Inequality Theorem

Theorem

The **Triangle Inequality Theorem** states that the sum of the lengths of any two sides of a triangle is greater than the length of the third side.

EXAMPLE

The "greater than" symbol, >, points at the lesser value.

A triangle has one side of length 15 and another of length 9. Describe the possible lengths of the third side.

Solution:

Let x represent the length of the third side. Draw diagrams to help visualize the small and large values of x. Then use the Triangle Inequality Theorem to write and solve inequalities.

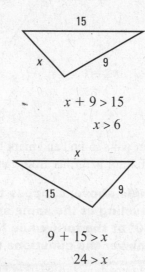

$$x + 9 > 15$$
$$x > 6$$

$$9 + 15 > x$$
$$24 > x$$

The length of the third side is greater than 6 but less than 24.

PRACTICE

You are given two side lengths of a triangle. Describe the possible lengths of the remaining side.

7. 22 feet and 36 feet   **8.** 19 yards and 6 yards   **9.** 2 inches and 3 inches

10. 53 miles and 3 miles   **11.** 2 cm and 6 cm   **12.** 7 m and 26 m

BENCHMARK 3
B. Inequalities in Triangles

BENCHMARK 3
(Chapters 5, 6, and 7)

3. Use the Hinge Theorem

Theorem

The **Hinge Theorem** states that if two sides of one triangle are congruent to two sides of another triangle, and the included angle of the first is larger than the included angle of the second, then the third side of the first is longer than the third side of the second.

EXAMPLE

The "hinge" in the Hinge Theorem is the included angle.

Two hikers walk north together from camp along a straight path for 4 miles until they come to a fork. Hiker *A* makes a 65° right turn at the fork while Hiker *B* takes an 85° turn to the left. They continue hiking separately with a speed of 1.5 miles per hour. Determine which hiker is closest to camp after 2 hours.

Solution:

Draw a diagram and mark the given distances and angle measures. The distances hiked and the distances back to camp form two triangles with congruent 4-mile sides and congruent 3-mile sides. Add the third sides of the triangles to your diagram.

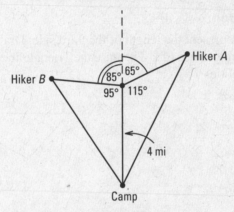

Next use linear pairs to find and mark the included angles of 95° and 115°. Because 115° > 95°, Hiker *A* is further from camp than Hiker *B* by the Hinge Theorem.

PRACTICE

In the example above, suppose there are two other people, Hiker *C* and Hiker *D*, traveling at the same speed with the other two and that Hiker *C* turns left 70° at the fork while Hiker *D* continues in a straight line past the fork. Answer the questions that follow.

13. After 3 hours, how far is Hiker *D* from camp?

14. After 3 hours, who is closest to camp? Furthest from camp?

15. Who is closer to camp after 4 hours, Hiker *B* or Hiker *C*?

16. Who is further from camp after 5 hours, Hiker *C* or Hiker *D*?

17. Arrange the hikers from closest to furthest from camp after 8 hours have elapsed.

BENCHMARK 3
(Chapters 5, 6, and 7)

4. Write an Indirect Proof

Vocabulary

An **indirect proof** assumes the desired conclusion is false and reaches a logical impossibility, thus showing this assumption is incorrect so that the desired conclusion is in fact true.

EXAMPLE

Be sure you are assuming the desired conclusion is false and not the given hypotheses.

Write an indirect proof that no two consecutive integers are both divisible by 5.

Given: n and $n + 1$ are consecutive integers.

Prove: n and $n + 1$ are not both divisible by 5.

Solution:

Step 1: Assume temporarily that both n and $n + 1$ are divisible by 5. Then $\frac{n}{5} = m_1$ and $\frac{n + 1}{5} = m_2$ for some integers m_1 and m_2. Multiplying both sides of each equation gives $n = 5m_1$ and $n + 1 = 5m_2$.

Step 2: Solving each equation for n gives $n = 5m_1$ and $n + 1 = 5m_2$. By substitution, we have that $5m_1 = 5m_2 - 1$. This can not be a true equation since the left hand side is a multiple of 5 while the right hand side is not.

Step 3: Therefore, the assumption that both n and $n + 1$ were both divisible by 5 must be false, which proves that n and $n + 1$ are not both divisible by 5.

PRACTICE

Suppose you are writing an indirect proof of the theorem listed. State the conclusion that you are temporarily assuming.

18. Theorem 5.10

19. Theorem 5.11

20. The Triangle Inequality Theorem

21. The Converse of the Hinge Theorem

Quiz

1. Describe the possible lengths of the third side of a triangle if the other two sides have lengths:

    a. 8 and 12   **b.** 14 and 35

2. List the lengths of the sides of $\triangle ABC$ from shortest to longest if:

    a. $m\angle A = 35°$, $m\angle B = 18°$, $m\angle C = 127°$

    b. $m\angle A = x°$, $m\angle B = 3x°$, $m\angle C = 2x°$

BENCHMARK 3
B. Inequalities in Triangles

BENCHMARK 3
(Chapters 5, 6, and 7)

3. Use the Hinge Theorem to decide which is larger, *AC* or *AD*.

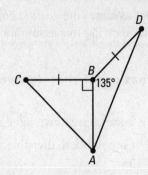

4. In order to write an indirect proof of the fact that the sum of two odd integers is an even integer, what is the conclusion you must temporarily assume?

Name _____   Date _____

BENCHMARK 3
(Chapters 5, 6, and 7)

C. Similarity and Proportionality Theorems

You can use similarity to measure lengths indirectly. For example, you can use similar triangles to find the height of a tree.

1. Use Similar Polygons

Vocabulary

Two polygons are **similar** if corresponding angles are congruent and corresponding side lengths are proportional. The ratio of the lengths of corresponding sides is called the **scale factor**.

EXAMPLE

In the diagram, $\triangle DEF \sim \triangle MNP$. Find the value of x and the scale factor.

There are several different ways to write the proportion. For example,

$$\frac{DE}{MN} = \frac{EF}{NP}.$$

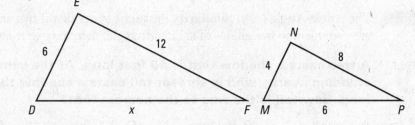

Solution:

The triangles are similar, so the corresponding side lengths are proportional.

$\dfrac{DE}{MN} = \dfrac{DF}{MP}.$	**Write the proportion.**
$\dfrac{6}{4} = \dfrac{x}{6}$	**Substitute.**
$36 = 4x$	**Cross Products Property**
$x = 9$	**Solve for x.**

To find the scale factor, find the ratio of the lengths of a pair of corresponding sides.

For example, $\dfrac{DE}{MN} = \dfrac{6}{4} = 1.5$. The scale factor is 1.5.

PRACTICE   **Find the scale factor for each pair of similar figures and the value of x.**

1.

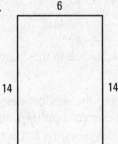

2.

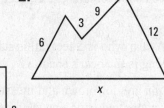
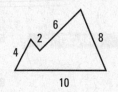

BENCHMARK 3
(Chapters 5, 6, and 7)

3.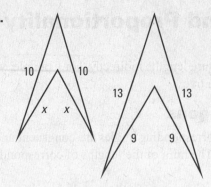

4.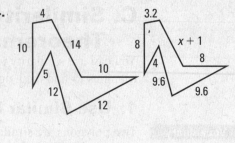

2. Use AA Similarity

Postulate The **Angle-Angle (AA) Similarity Postulate** states that if two angles of one triangle are congruent to two angles of another triangle, then the two triangles are similar.

EXAMPLE

Notice that the man's height is taller than his shadow so that the tree's height must be taller than its shadow. Thus we can omit choices A and D immediately.

A tree casts a shadow that is 40 feet long. At the same time, a man standing nearby who is six feet tall casts a shadow that is 48 inches long. How tall is the tree to the nearest foot?

A. 25 feet   **B.** 60 feet   **C.** 100 feet   **D.** 35 feet

Solution:

The tree and the man form sides of two right triangles with the ground, as shown below. The sun's rays hit the tree and the man at the same angle. You have two pairs of congruent angles, so the triangles are Similar by the AA Similarity Postulate.

We can use a proportion to find the height *x*.
Write six feet as 72 inches so that you can form two ratios of feet to inches.

$$\frac{x \text{ ft}}{72 \text{ in.}} = \frac{40 \text{ ft}}{48 \text{ in.}}$$ **Write proportion of side lengths.**

$48x = 72(40)$ **Cross Products Property**

$x = 60$ **Solve for *x*.**

The tree is 60 feet tall. The correct answer is B.

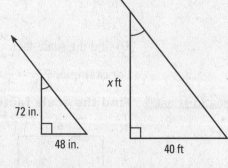

PRACTICE

5. A bear who is 5 feet tall is standing next to the tree in the example above. How long is the bear's shadow?

6. You are downtown and measure the lengths of the shadow cast by a tall sky-scraper and your own shadow as you stand. Set up a proportion that could be solved in order to estimate the height of the skyscraper. Let *h* and *s* represent your height and your shadow's length, respectively, and *H* and *S* the height of the skyscraper and the length of its shadow, respectively.

7. Suppose your friend, who is much shorter than you, estimates the height of the same skyscraper in the same way but at a different time of day. Is it likely that his estimate will be close to yours? Explain.

**BENCHMARK 3
C. Similarity**

BENCHMARK 3
(Chapters 5, 6, and 7)

3. Use SSS Similarity

Theorem   The **Side-Side-Side (SSS) Similarity Theorem** states that if the corresponding side lengths of two triangles are proportional, then the triangles are similar.

EXAMPLE   **Find the value of *x* that makes △*ABC* ~ △*DEF*.**

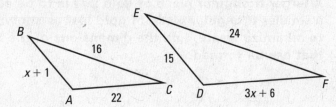

When using the SSS Similarity Theorem, compare the shortest sides, the longest sides, and then the remaining sides.

Solution:

Step 1: Find the value of *x* that makes corresponding sides lengths proportional.

$$\frac{16}{24} = \frac{22}{3x + 6}$$ **Write proportion.**

$16 \cdot (3x + 6) = 24 \cdot 22$ **Cross Products Property**

$48x + 96 = 528$ **Simplify.**

$x = 9$ **Solve for *x*.**

Step 2: Check that the side lengths are proportional when $x = 9$.

$BA = x + 1 = 10$ $DF = 3x + 6 = 33$

$\frac{BC}{EF} \overset{?}{=} \frac{BA}{ED} : \frac{16}{24} = \frac{10}{15}$ TRUE $\frac{BC}{EF} \overset{?}{=} \frac{CA}{DF} : \frac{16}{24} = \frac{22}{33}$ TRUE

When $x = 9$, the triangles are similar by the SSS Similarity Theorem.

PRACTICE   **Refer to the triangles shown.**

8. Name two pairs of similar triangles.

9. The shortest side of a triangle similar to △*LMN* is 6 units long. Find the other side lengths of the triangle.

10. The longest side of a triangle similar to △*ABC* is 6 units long. Find the other side lengths of the triangle.

11. The shortest side of a triangle similar to △*RST* is 9 units long. Find the other side lengths of the triangle.

12. The shortest side of a triangle similar to △*RST* is *x* units long and the longest side is $2x - 1$ units long. Find the shortest and longest side lengths of the triangle.

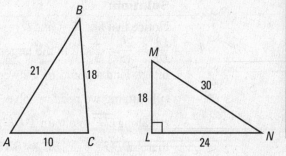

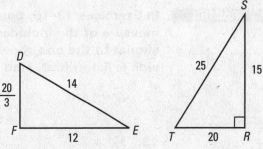

BENCHMARK 3
C. Similarity

Name _____   Date _____

BENCHMARK 3
(Chapters 5, 6, and 7)

4. Use SAS Similarity

Theorem The **Side-Angle-Side (SAS) Similarity Theorem** states that if an angle of one triangle is congruent to an angle of a second and the lengths of the sides including these angles are proportional, then the triangles are similar.

EXAMPLE **A larger triangular piece of gold leaf is to be cut so that it is similar to a smaller triangular piece of gold leaf as shown in the diagram. In order to minimize waste, find the dimensions of the largest similar triangle that can be formed.**

We can cut from a point on side $\overline{DF}$ to E to construct a similar triangle, but since we want the *biggest* triangle we don't want to shorten the longest side of $\triangle DEF$ if we do not have to.

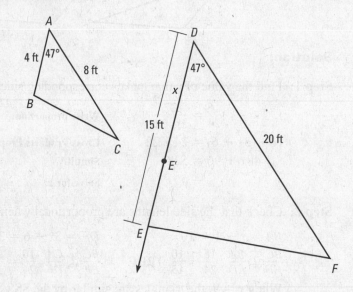

Solution:

Notice that $m\angle A = m\angle D = 47°$. Since $\dfrac{AC}{AB} = \dfrac{8}{4} = 2$ in the smaller triangle and $\dfrac{DF}{DE} = \dfrac{20}{15} = \dfrac{4}{3} < 2$ in the larger triangle, we should shorten side $\overline{DE}$ while keeping $\overline{DF}$ intact. Find a point, E', between D and E so that $\dfrac{DF}{DE'} = 2$. Letting $x = DE'$ and substituting we need to solve $\dfrac{20}{x} = 2$ for x. It is easy to see that $x = 10$. So we need to cut along $\overline{E'F}$ to obtain $\triangle DE'F$. We check $\dfrac{AB}{DE'} \stackrel{?}{=} \dfrac{AC}{DF} : \dfrac{4}{10} = \dfrac{8}{20}$ TRUE. So we know that $\triangle DE'F \sim \triangle ABC$ by SAS Similarity Theorem.

PRACTICE **In Exercises 13–15, two side lengths and the measure of the included angle of a triangle similar to the one shown are given. The shorter side is listed first. Find the value of *x*.**

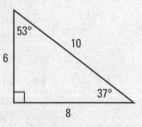

13. $53°, x, 2x - 3$ **14.** $37°, x + 1, 2x - 1$ **15.** $90°, 2x - 1, x + 4$

16. Could a triangle with sides of length 3 and 4 with an included angle of 37° be similar to the given triangle?

BENCHMARK 3
(Chapters 5, 6, and 7)

5. Dilations

EXAMPLE   Pentagon *ABCDE* is similar to pentagon *FGHJE*. Describe the dilation that moves *ABCDE* onto *FGHJE*.

Solution:

The figure shows a dilation with center *E*.

The scale factor is the ratio of the lengths of corresponding sides.

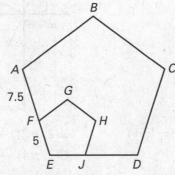

The ratio of the sides is $\frac{EF}{EA} = \frac{5}{12.5} = \frac{2}{5}$, so the scale factor is $\frac{2}{5}$.

PRACTICE   **Give the dilation factor of the transformations below.**

17. A 4" x 6" picture enlarged to 12" x 18".

18. A scale model with a height of 2' and a width of 3' is used to build a house that is 30' tall and 45' wide.

19. △*ABC* to △*AED*

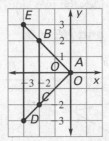

6. Draw a Dilation

Vocabulary   The **scale factor of a dilation** is the ratio of a side length of the image to the corresponding side length of the original figure.

EXAMPLE   Draw a dilation of quadrilateral *ABCD* with vertices *A*(2, −2), *B*(4, 2), *C*(2, −4), and *D*(0, 0). Use a scale factor of 1.5.

BENCHMARK 3
(Chapters 5, 6, and 7)

Photo enlargements are dilations.

Solution:

First draw *ABCD*. Find the dilation of each vertex by multiplying its coordinates by 1.5. Then draw the dilation.

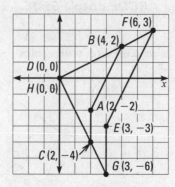

$(x, y) \rightarrow (1.5x, 1.5y)$ $A(2, -2) \rightarrow E(3, -3)$ $B(4, 2) \rightarrow F(6, 3)$

$C(2, -4) \rightarrow G(3, -6)$ $D(0, 0) \rightarrow H(0, 0)$

PRACTICE   **Find the coordinates of *L, M,* and *N* so that △*LMN* is a dilation of △*PQR* with a scale factor of *K*. Sketch △*PQR* and △*LMN*.**

20. $P(-3, 1), Q(0, 2), R(2, -4); k = 2$ **21.** $P(2, -2), Q(3, -2), R(-2, -4); k = 0.5$

22. $P(6, 3), Q(3, 0), R(-9, 6); k = \frac{1}{3}$ **23.** $P(5, -2), Q(7, -4), R(12, -6); k = 5$

7. Use Triangle Proportionality

Theorem   The **Triangle Proportionality Theorem** states that if a line parallel to one side of a triangle intersects the other two sides, then it divides the two sides proportionally.

EXAMPLE   **In the diagram, $\overline{GH} \parallel \overline{DE}$, GF = 3, FH = 4, and HE = 8.**

Find the length of $\overline{DG}$.

Review properties of proportions in section 6.2.

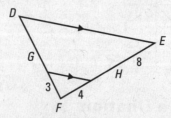

Solution:

We have that $\frac{FG}{GD} = \frac{FH}{HE}$ by the Triangle Proportionality Theorem. By substitution we obtain: $\frac{3}{DG} = \frac{4}{8}$. Next, we cross-multiply to get $3 \cdot 8 = 4 \cdot DG$. Divide both sides by 4 and simplify to see that $DG = 6$.

BENCHMARK 3
C. Similarity

Name _____ Date _____

BENCHMARK 3
(Chapters 5, 6, and 7)

PRACTICE Use the Triangle Proportionality Theorem to solve for *x* in each case.

24.
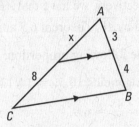

25.
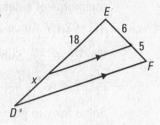

26.
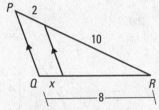

27.
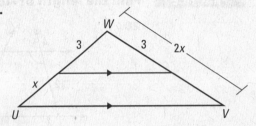

8. Use Proportionality Theorems

EXAMPLE

Review parallel lines in Lesson 3.3.

In the diagram, $\overline{QP} \parallel \overline{MN}$, $\angle BAC$ is bisected by $\overline{AV}$, *M* is the midpoint of side $\overline{AB}$, *N* is the midpoint of side $\overline{AC}$, $AM = 7$, $MP = 4$, $NQ = 3$, and $BC = 12$.

a. Find AN.

b. Find BV.

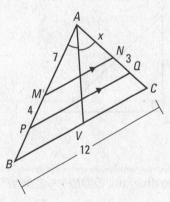

Solution:

a. Notice that since $\overline{MN}$ is a midsegment of $\triangle ABC$, we have that $\overline{MN} \parallel \overline{BC}$. Since we are given that $\overline{QP} \parallel \overline{MN}$, we must also have that $\overline{QP} \parallel \overline{BC}$, by the transitive property of parallel lines. Thus Theorem 6.6 applies and we can say that

$\frac{AM}{PM} = \frac{AN}{NQ}$. Letting $AN = x$ and substituting the given lengths, we obtain $\frac{7}{4} = \frac{x}{3}$, or $7 \cdot 3 = 4 \cdot x$, by the Cross Products Property. Solving for *x* we obtain

$x = \frac{21}{4}$. Thus $AN = \frac{21}{4} = 5.25$.

BENCHMARK 3
(Chapters 5, 6, and 7)

b. Letting $BV = y$, we have that $VC = 12 - y$. Notice that since N and M are the midpoints of sides $\overline{AC}$ and $\overline{AB}$, respectively, we have that $AB = 2AM$ and $AC = 2AN$. Since $\angle BAC$ is bisected by $\overline{AV}$, Theorem 6.7 applies to $\triangle ABC$ so that $\dfrac{BV}{VC} = \dfrac{AB}{AC}$. Substitution gives the following proportion: $\dfrac{y}{12 - y} = \dfrac{2 \cdot 7}{2 \cdot (5.25)}$. Cross multiplying yields $10.5y = 14(12 - y)$. Solve for y to get $y = \dfrac{48}{7}$. Thus $BV = \dfrac{48}{7} \approx 6.9$.

PRACTICE   **Find the length of $\overline{AB}$ in each case.**

28.

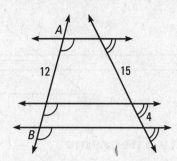

29.

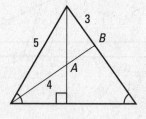

30.

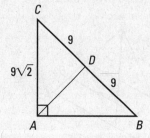

Quiz

1. In the diagram, $\triangle DEF \sim \triangle MNP$. Find the value of x and the scale factor.

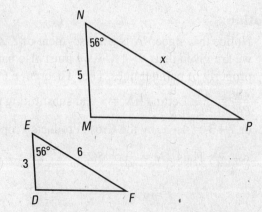

Geometry

BENCHMARK 3
(Chapters 5, 6, and 7)

2. A man, who is 6 feet tall, is standing 3 feet from his young son. The man casts a shadow on the ground which is 8 feet in length, the tip of which is aligned with the tip of the boy's shadow. How tall is the boy?

3. Name a pair of similar triangles and the postulate or theorem that justifies that assertion.

a.

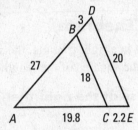

b.

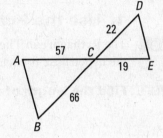

c.

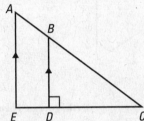

4. The two figures are similar. Describe the transformation from the smaller figure to the larger figure.

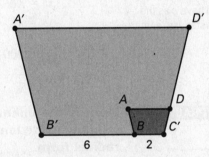

5. Draw a dilation of the pentagon $ABCDE$ with vertices $A(1, 3)$, $B(4, 0)$, $C(-2, 2)$, $D(-3, 3)$, and $E(0, 5)$. Use a scale factor of 2.

6. Find the length of $\overline{AB}$.

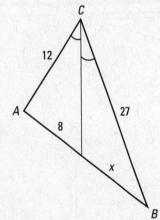

BENCHMARK 3
(Chapters 5, 6, and 7)

D. Pythagorean Theorem and Right Triangles

One of the most famous theorems in mathematics is the Pythagorean Theorem. This theorem can be used to find information about the lengths of the sides of a right triangle. We also investigate pairs of similar triangles found within right triangles.

1. Use the Pythagorean Theorem

Theorem The **Pythagorean Theorem** states that in a right triangle, the square of the length of the hypotenuse is equal to the sum of the squares of the lengths of the legs.

EXAMPLE **Find the length of the hypotenuse of the right triangle.**

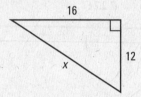

Not all right triangles with side lengths a, b, and c will have c as the hypotenuse length.

Solution:

$(\text{hypotenuse})^2 = (\text{leg})^2 + (\text{leg})^2$	**Pythagorean Theorem**
$x^2 = 16^2 + 12^2$	**Substitute.**
$x^2 = 256 + 122$	**Multiply.**
$x^2 = 400$	**Add.**
$x = 20$	**Find the positive square root.**

PRACTICE **Identify the unknown side as a leg or hypotenuse. Then, find the unknown side length of the right triangle. Write your answer in simplest radical form.**

1.

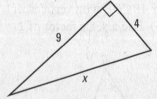

2.

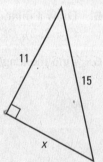

3.

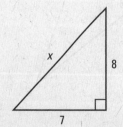

4.

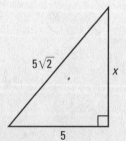

BENCHMARK 3
(Chapters 5, 6, and 7)

2. Use Common Pythagorean Triples

Vocabulary A **Pythagorean triple** is a set of three positive integers a, b, and c that satisfy the equation $c^2 = a^2 + b^2$.

EXAMPLE   **Find the length of the leg of the right triangle.**

Common Pythagorean triples are listed on page 435 of your text.

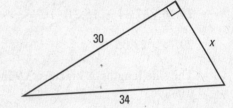

Solution:

Use a Pythagorean triple. A common Pythagorean triple is 8, 15, 17. Notice that if you multiply the lengths of the longer leg and the hypotenuse in this triple by two, you get the lengths of the longer leg and the hypotenuse of this triangle: 15 • 2 = 30 and 17 • 2 = 34. So, the length of the shorter leg of this triangle is 8 • 2 = 16.

PRACTICE   **Find the unknown side length of the right triangle by using a Pythagorean triple.**

5.

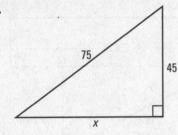

6.

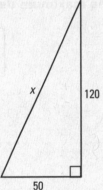

7.

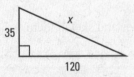

8.

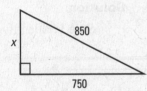

3. Classify Triangles

EXAMPLE   **Can the segments with length 2.8 inches, 3.9 inches, and 5.4 inches form a triangle? If so, would the triangle be acute, right, or obtuse?**

Solution:

The converse of the Pythagorean Theorem is also true.

Step 1: Use the Triangle Inequality Theorem to check that the segments can make a triangle.

2.8 + 3.9 = 6.7	2.8 + 5.4 = 8.2	3.9 + 5.4 = 9.3
6.7 > 5.4	8.2 > 3.9	9.3 > 2.8

The side lengths 2.8 inches, 3.9 inches, and 5.4 inches can form a triangle.

BENCHMARK 3
D. Pythagorean Theorem

BENCHMARK 3
(Chapters 5, 6, and 7)

Step 2: Classify the triangle by comparing the square of the length of the longest side with the sum of the squares of the shorter sides.

$c^2 \overset{?}{=} a^2 + b^2$ **Compare c^2 with $a^2 + b^2$.**

$5.4^2 \overset{?}{=} 2.8^2 + 3.9^2$ **Substitute.**

$29.16 \overset{?}{=} 7.84 + 15.21$ **Simplify.**

$29.16 > 23.05$ **c^2 is greater than $a^2 + b^2$.**

The side lengths 2.8 inches, 3.9 inches, and 5.4 inches form an obtuse triangle.

PRACTICE   **Segments with the lengths given form a triangle. Classify the triangle as acute, right, or obtuse.**

9. 7, 8, 9   **10.** 12, 12, 13   **11.** 48, 26, 70   **12.** 32.1, 43.9, 67.2

4. Use Altitudes of Right Triangles.

EXAMPLE   **The diagram below shows a cross-section of a swimming pool. What is the maximum depth of the pool?**

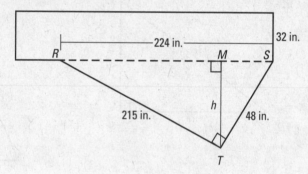

Solution:

     Step 1: Identify the similar triangles and sketch them.

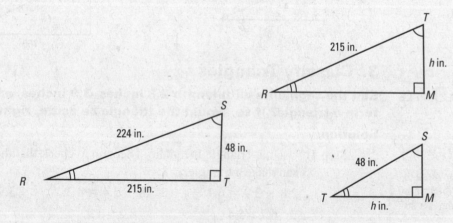

$\triangle RST \sim \triangle RTM \sim \triangle TSM.$

BENCHMARK 3
(Chapters 5, 6, and 7)

Step 2: Find the value of h. Use the fact that $\triangle RST$, $\triangle RTM$ to write a proportion.

$$\frac{TM}{ST} = \frac{TR}{SR}$$ **Corresponding side lengths of similar triangles are in proportion.**

Be sure to set up a proportion that you can actually solve.

$$\frac{h}{48} = \frac{215}{224}$$ **Substitute.**

$$224h = 48(215)$$ **Cross Products Property**

$$h \approx 46.1$$ **Solve for h.**

Step 3: Read the diagram above. You can see that the maximum depth of the pool is $h + 32$, which is about 78.1 inches.

PRACTICE   **Identify the similar triangles. Then find the value of x. Round decimal answers to the nearest tenth.**

13.

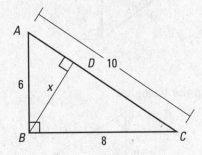

14.

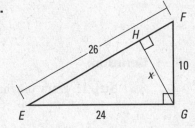

15.

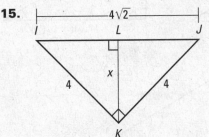

16.

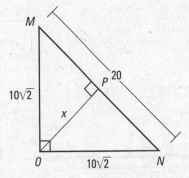

BENCHMARK 3
D. Pythagorean Theorem

BENCHMARK 3
(Chapters 5, 6, and 7)

5. Use Geometric Means

EXAMPLE

Review Theorems 7.6 and 7.7 on page 452 of your text.

To find the cost of installing a rock wall in your school gym, you need to find the height of the gym wall. You use a square to line up the top and the bottom of the wall. Your friend measures the vertical distance from the floor to your eye and the distance from you to the wall as recorded in the diagram. Approximate the height of the wall.

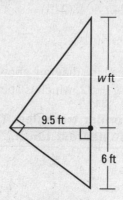

Solution:

Step 1: Draw the three similar triangles.

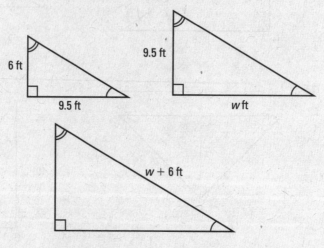

Step 2: Write a proportion.

$$\frac{6}{9.5} = \frac{9.5}{w}$$

Step 3: Solve the proportion.

$6w = 9.5(9.5)$ **Cross Products Property**

$w = \dfrac{(9.5)^2}{6}$ **Multiply and divide.**

$w \approx 15.04$ **Simplify.**

So, the height of the wall is $6 + w \approx 21.04$ feet.

BENCHMARK 3
D. Pythagorean Theorem

BENCHMARK 3
(Chapters 5, 6, and 7)

PRACTICE   Various people measure the same wall as in the example above.
Tell how far each must stand from the wall if their eyes are the
given distance off the floor.

17. A basketball player: 7 feet

18. A mascot: 4 feet

19. A cheerleader on the top of a pyramid: 18 feet

20. How far off the ground are the eyes of a person who must stand the furthest
from the wall in order to measure it in this way?

6. Find Lengths of Special Right Triangles

Vocabulary   A **45°-45°-90° triangle** is an isosceles right triangle, which can be formed by cutting a
square in half along its diagonal. A **30°-60°-90° triangle** can be formed by cutting an
equilateral triangle along one of its altitudes.

Find the value of *x* in each case. Write your answer in simplest radical form.

You should
memorize the
proportions of
a 45°-45°-90°
triangle and a
30°-60°-90°
triangle.

a.

b.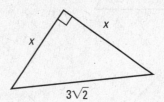

c.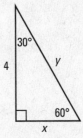

Solution:

a. By the Triangle Sum Theorem, the measure of the third angle must be 45° so
this is a 45°-45°-90° triangle and Theorem 7.8 tells us that the length of the
hypotenuse is $\sqrt{2}$ times the length of the leg. Thus $x = 6\sqrt{2}$.

b. By the Base Angles Theorem and the Corollary to the Triangle Sum Theorem, the
triangle is a 45°-45°-90° triangle, so the length of the hypotenuse is $\sqrt{2}$ times the
length of each leg. Thus, $3\sqrt{2} = \sqrt{2} \cdot x$. Solving for *x* we obtain $x = 3$.

c. First, find the value of *x*, the shorter leg.

longer leg = shorter leg · $\sqrt{3}$	**30°-60°-90° Triangle Theorem**
$4 = x \cdot \sqrt{3}$	**Substitute.**
$\dfrac{4}{\sqrt{3}} \cdot \dfrac{\sqrt{3}}{\sqrt{3}} = x$	**Divide both sides by $\sqrt{3}$; multiply numerator and denominator by $\sqrt{3}$.**
$\dfrac{4\sqrt{3}}{3} = x$	**Simplify.**

**BENCHMARK 3
D. Pythagorean Theorem**

BENCHMARK 3
(Chapters 5, 6, and 7)

Next, find the value of y, the hypotenuse:

hypotenuse = 2 • shorter leg   **30°-60°-90° Triangle Theorem**

$$y = 2 \cdot \frac{4\sqrt{3}}{3}$$ **Substitute.**

$$y = \frac{8\sqrt{3}}{3}$$ **Simplify.**

PRACTICE   **Find the value of the variables. Write your answer is simplest radical form.**

21.
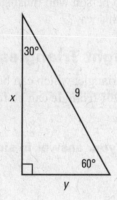

22.
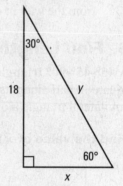

23.
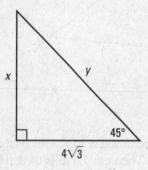

24.
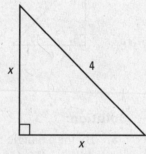

Quiz

1. Identify the unknown side as a leg or hypotenuse. Then, find the unknown side length of the right triangle. Write your answer in simplest radical form.

   a.
   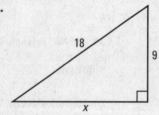

   b.
   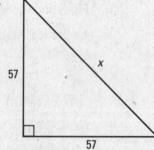

BENCHMARK 3
D. Pythagorean Theorem

BENCHMARK 3
(Chapters 5, 6, and 7)

2. Find the unknown side length of the right triangle by using a Pythagorean triple.

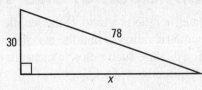

3. Segments with the lengths given form a triangle. Classify the triangle as acute, right, or obtuse.

a. 57, 98, 129

b. 102, 129, 213

In Exercises 4–6, identify the similar triangles and solve a proportion to find *x* in each case.

4.

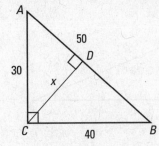

5.

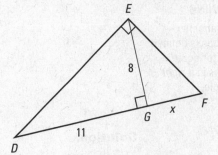

6.

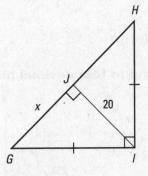

7. Find *x* and *y*.

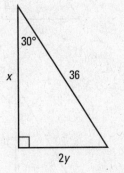

8. Find *x* and *y*.

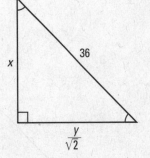

BENCHMARK 3
(Chapters 5, 6, and 7)

E. Sine, Cosine, and Tangent

A trigonometric ratio is a ratio of the lengths of two sides in a right triangle. You will use trigonometric ratios to find the measure of a side or an acute angle in a right triangle. You can use such ratios to measure objects, such as mountains or tall buildings, indirectly.

1. Find Tangent Ratios

Vocabulary   Given an acute angle in a right triangle, the **tangent** of this angle is the ratio of the length of the side opposite the angle to the length of the side adjacent to the angle. If the angle is α then we denote its tangent by tan α.

EXAMPLE

WARNING:
The tangent function is defined here for acute angles in a *right* triangle.

Find tan *S* and tan *R*. Write each answer as a fraction and as a decimal rounded to four places.

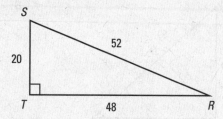

Solution:

$$\tan S = \frac{opp. \angle S}{adj. \text{ to } \angle S} = \frac{RT}{ST} = \frac{48}{20} = \frac{12}{5} = 2.4$$

$$\tan R = \frac{opp. \angle R}{adj. \text{ to } \angle R} = \frac{ST}{RT} = \frac{20}{48} = \frac{5}{12} = 0.4167$$

PRACTICE   **Find the tangent of *J* and *K*. Round to four decimal places.**

1.
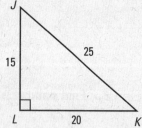

2.
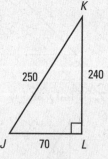

3.
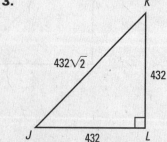

4.
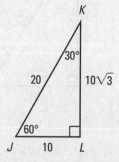

BENCHMARK 3
E. Sine, Cosine, and Tangent

BENCHMARK 3
(Chapters 5, 6, and 7)

2. Find a Length Using Tangent

EXAMPLE

Make sure your calculator is in degree mode.

Find the height *h* of the building to the nearest foot.

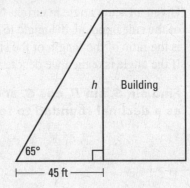

Solution:

$\tan 65° = \dfrac{opp.}{adj.}$ **Write the ratio for tangent of 65°.**

$\tan 65° = \dfrac{h}{45}$ **Substitute.**

$45 \cdot \tan 65° = h$ **Multiply each side by 45.**

$96.5 \approx h$ **Use a calculator to simplify.**

The building is about 97 feet tall.

PRACTICE **Find the value of *x*. Round to the nearest tenth.**

5.

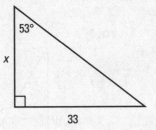

6.

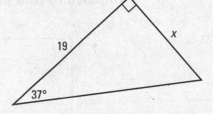

7.

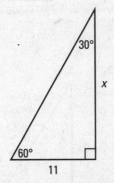

8.

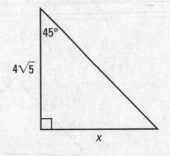

BENCHMARK 3
E. Sine, Cosine, and Tangent

BENCHMARK 3
(Chapters 5, 6, and 7)

3. Find Sine and Cosine Ratios

Vocabulary   Given an acute angle in a right triangle, the **sine** of this angle is the ratio of the length of the side opposite the angle to the length of the hypotenuse. The **cosine** of this angle is the ratio of the length of the side adjacent to the angle to the length of the hypotenuse. If the angle is α then we denote its sine by sin α and its cosine by cos α.

EXAMPLE   **Find sin S, sin R, cos S, and cos R. Write each answer as a fraction and as a decimal rounded to four places.**

SOHCAHTOA
Sine:
Opposite
Hypotenuse
Cosine:
Adjacent
Hypotenuse
Tangent:
Opposite
Adjacent

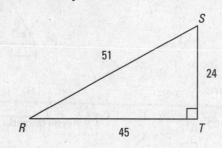

Solution:

$$\sin S = \frac{opp. \angle S}{hyp.} = \frac{45}{51} \approx 0.8824 \qquad \sin R = \frac{opp. \angle R}{hyp.} = \frac{24}{51} \approx 0.4706$$

$$\cos S = \frac{adj. \text{ to } \angle S}{hyp.} = \frac{24}{51} \approx 0.4706 \qquad \cos R = \frac{adj. \text{ to } \angle R}{hyp.} = \frac{45}{51} \approx 0.8824$$

PRACTICE   **Find sin S and cos S. Write each answer as a fraction and as a decimal rounded to four places.**

9.

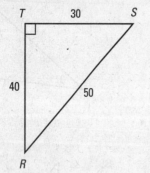

10.

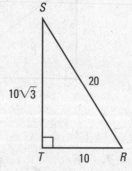

11.

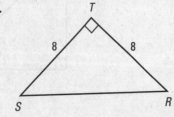

12.

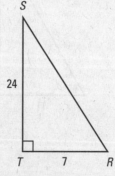

BENCHMARK 3
(Chapters 5, 6, and 7)

4. Use Angles of Elevation and Depression

Vocabulary

If you look up at an object, the angle your line of sight makes with a horizontal line is called **the angle of elevation**. If you look down at an object, the angle your line of sight makes with a horizontal line is called **the angle of depression**.

EXAMPLE

Angles of elevation slant up while angles of depression slant down.

A fireman climbs on a ladder with an angle of elevation of 72°. The bottom of the ladder is 10 feet from the base of a building. The top of the ladder reaches an open window where a cat waits to be rescued.

a. Use the angle of elevation to calculate the length of the ladder.

b. Use an angle of depression to calculate the height of the window.

Solution:

a. $\cos 72° = \dfrac{adj.}{hyp.}$ Write ratio for cosine of 72°.

$\cos 72° = \dfrac{10}{\ell}$ Substitute.

$\ell \cdot \cos 72° = 10$ Multiply each side by ℓ.

$\ell = \dfrac{10}{\cos 72°}$ Divide each side by cos 72°.

$\ell \approx \dfrac{10}{0.3090}$ Use a calculator to find cos 72°.

$\ell \approx 32.4$ Simplify.

The ladder is about 32.4 feet long.

b. By the Triangle Sum Theorem, the angle of depression is $180° - (90° + 72°) = 18°$.

$\tan 72° = \dfrac{opp.}{adj.}$ Write ratio for tangent of 18°.

$\tan 18° = \dfrac{10}{h}$ Substitute.

$h \cdot \tan 18° = 10$ Multiply each side by h.

$h = \dfrac{10}{\tan 18°}$ Divide each side by tan 18°.

$h \approx \dfrac{10}{0.3249}$ Use a calculator to find tan 18°.

$h \approx 30.8$ Simplify.

The window is about 30.8 feet above the ground.

PRACTICE

Find the length of the ladder and the height of the window as in the example above if the angle of elevation and distance from the ladder to the base of the building are as given below.

13. 72°, 5 feet

14. 72°, 20 feet

15. 36°, 10 feet

16. 36°, 20 feet

BENCHMARK 3
E. Sine, Cosine, and Tangent

BENCHMARK 3
(Chapters 5, 6, and 7)

17. Describe how the lengths given and found in 13 and 14 are related to the lengths given and found in the example.

18. Does halving the angle of elevation, as in 15 and 16, halve the length of the ladder or the height of the window?

5. Use Inverse Trigonometric Ratios

Vocabulary

Let A be an acute angle. If $\tan A = x$, then $\tan^{-1} x = m\angle A$. If $\sin A = x$, then $\sin^{-1} x = m\angle A$. If $\cos A = x$, then $\cos^{-1} x = m\angle A$. These ratios are called the **inverse tangent, inverse sine** and **inverse cosine**.

EXAMPLE

The inverse trigonometric ratios have only been defined for acute angles at this stage.

a. Use a calculator to approximate the measure of $\angle A$ to the nearest tenth of a degree.

b. Let $\angle D$ and $\angle E$ be acute angles in a right triangles ABD and EFH. Use a calculator to approximate the measure of $\angle D$ and $\angle E$ to the nearest tenth of a degree if $\sin D = 0.1234$ and $\cos E = 0.8888$.

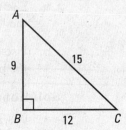

Solution:

a. Because $\tan A = \dfrac{12}{9} = \dfrac{4}{3} \approx 1.333$, $\tan^{-1} 1.3333 \approx m\angle A$. Using a calculator, $\tan^{-1} 1.3333 \approx 53.12941479\ldots$. So, the measure of $\angle A$ is approximately $53.1°$.

b. $m\angle D = \sin^{-1} 0.1234 \approx 7.1°$ and $m\angle E = \cos^{-1} 0.8888 \approx 27.3°$.

PRACTICE

Find the measure of $\angle C$ in each case. Round to the nearest tenth of a degree.

19. $\tan C = 0.4767$ **20.** $\sin C = 0.2079$ **21.** $\cos C = 0.6081$

22. $\tan C = 0.5196$ **23.** $\sin C = 0.8047$ **24.** $\cos C = 0.0046$

6. Solve a Right Triangle

Vocabulary

To **solve a right triangle** means to find the measures of all its sides and angles.

EXAMPLE

Recall that the two acute angles in a right triangle are complementary.

Solve the right triangle. Round decimal answers to the nearest tenth.

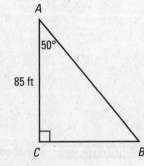

Solution:

Step 1: Find $m\angle B$ by using the Triangle Sum Theorem:

$$m\angle B = 180° - (90° + 50°)$$
$$m\angle B = 40°$$

Step 2: Approximate BC by using a tangent ratio

$\tan 50° = \dfrac{BC}{85}$	**Write ratio for tangent of 50°.**
$85 \cdot \tan 50° = BC$	**Multiply each side by 85.**
$85 \cdot 1.1918 = BC$	**Use a calculator to find tan 50°.**
$101.3 \approx BC$	**Simplify and round answer.**

BENCHMARK 3
(Chapters 5, 6, and 7)

Step 3: Approximate *AB* by using a cosine ratio.

$$\cos 50° = \frac{85}{AB}$$ **Write ratio for cosine of 50°.**

$$AB \cdot \cos 50° = 85$$ **Multiply each side by *AB*.**

$$AB = \frac{85}{\cos 50°}$$ **Divide each side by cos 50°.**

$$AB \approx \frac{85}{0.6428}$$ **Use a calculator to find cos 50°.**

$$132.2 \approx AB$$ **Simplify.**

Thus, the angle measures are 40°, 50°, and 90°, and the side lengths are 85 feet, 101.3 feet, and 132.2 feet.

PRACTICE   **Solve the right triangle. Round decimal answers to the nearest tenth.**

25.

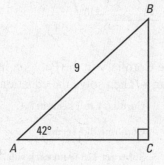

26.

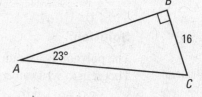

27.

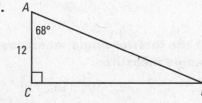

Quiz

In Exercises 1–6, refer to the diagram. Give decimal answers to four decimal places.

1. Find tan ∠*A*.

2. Find cos ∠*B*.

3. Find tan ∠*ACD*.

4. Find *m*∠*B*.

5. Find *m*∠*A*.

6. Find *m*∠*ACD*.

7. You are standing on level ground and look up at a sign on a wall at an angle of elevation of 20°. The sign is 15 feet higher than the height of your eyes. How far are you standing from the wall?

BENCHMARK 3
E. Sine, Cosine, and Tangent

BENCHMARK 4
(Chapters 8 and 9)

A. Parallelograms

We investigate properties of parallelograms and learn when a quadrilateral is a parallelogram.

1. Find an Unknown Interior Angle Measure

Theorem The **Polygon Interior Angles Theorem** states that the sum of the measures of the interior angles of a convex n-gon is $(n - 2) \cdot 180°$.

EXAMPLE **Find the value of x in the diagram shown.**

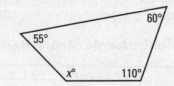

Solution:

The polygon is a quadrilateral. Use the Corollary to the Polygon Interior Angles Theorem to write an equation involving x. Then solve the equation.

A quadrilateral is a 4-gon.

$$x + 55 + 60 + 110 = 360 \qquad \text{Corollary to Theorem 8.1.}$$

$$x + 225 = 360 \qquad \text{Combine like terms.}$$

$$x = 135 \qquad \text{Subtract 225 from each side.}$$

The value of x is 135.

PRACTICE **You are given all but one of the interior angle measures of a convex polygon. Find the missing angle measure.**

   1. 60°, 30°   **2.** 50°, 110°, 150°

   3. 90°, 90°, 120°, 175°   **4.** 75°, 85°, 100°, 150°, 175°

   5. 110°, 120°, 130°, 135°, 135°, 150°   **6.** 120°, 120°, 130°, 130°, 140°, 140°, 150°

2. Find Angle Measures in Regular Polygons

Vocabulary The angles which form linear pairs with the interior angles of a polygon are said to be **exterior angles**.

Memorize the formula from Theorem 8.1.

Theorem The **Polygon Exterior Angles Theorem** states that the sum of the measures of the exterior angles of a convex polygon, one angle at each vertex, is 360°.

BENCHMARK 4
(Chapters 8 and 9)

EXAMPLE **A window shaped like a regular octagon is sketched below. Find the following measures.**

a. Each interior angle   **b.** Each exterior angle

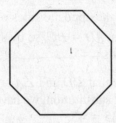

Solution:

a. Use the Polygon Interior Angles Theorem to find the measures of the interior angles.

$(n - 2) \cdot 180° = (8 - 2) \cdot 180° = 1080°$

Then find the measure of one interior angle. A regular octagon has 8 congruent interior angles. Divide 1080° by 8: $1080° \div 8 = 135°$. The measure of each interior angle in the octagon is 135°.

b. By the Polygon Exterior Angles Theorem, the sum of the measures of the exterior angles, one angle at each vertex, is 360°. Divide 360° by 8 to find the measure of one of the 8 congruent exterior angles: $360° \div 8 = 45°$. The measure of each exterior angle in the octagon is 45°.

PRACTICE **Find the measures of the interior and exterior angles of the regular polygon.**

7. pentagon   **8.** hexagon   **9.** heptagon

10. nonagon   **11.** decagon   **12.** 14-gon

3. Use Properties of Parallelograms

Vocabulary A **parallelogram** is a quadrilateral with both pairs of opposite sides parallel. In parallelogram $ABCD$, $AB \parallel CD$ and $BC \parallel DA$.

EXAMPLE **a.** Find the values of x, y, and z.

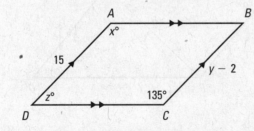

b. The diagonals of parallelogram $LMNO$ intersect at point P. Find the coordinates of P.

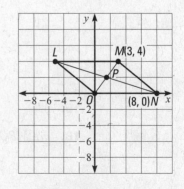

BENCHMARK 4
(Chapters 8 and 9)

Solution:

a. *ABCD* is a parallelogram by the definition of a parallelogram. By Theorem 8.4, $\angle C \cong \angle A$ so $m\angle C = m\angle A$. Thus $135° = x°$ so that $x = 135$.

By Theorem 8.3, the opposite sides of a parallelogram are congruent, so $\overline{AD} \cong \overline{BC}$. That is, $AD = BC$, so by substitution we get $15 = y - 2$. Adding 2 to both sides yields $y = 17$.

Finally, we notice that $\angle D$ and $\angle A$ are consecutive. By Theorem 8.5, $m\angle D + m\angle A = 180°$. By substitution, we have $z° + x° = 180°$. Since $x = 135$, this means that $z = 180 - 135 = 45$.

Recall the midpoint formula.

b. By Theorem 8.6, the diagonals of a parallelogram bisect each other. Since *P* is the point at which the diagonals of parallelogram *LMNO* intersect, we have that $\overline{LN}$ bisects $\overline{OM}$ and so *P* is the midpoint of $\overline{OM}$. We use the midpoint formula to find the coordinates of *P*: $\left(\dfrac{x_1 + x_2}{2}, \dfrac{y_1 + y_2}{2}\right) = \left(\dfrac{0 + 3}{2}, \dfrac{0 + 4}{2}\right) = \left(\dfrac{3}{2}, \dfrac{4}{2}\right) = \left(\dfrac{3}{2}, 2\right)$.

The coordinates of *P* are $\left(\dfrac{3}{2}, 2\right)$.

PRACTICE **Find the values of *x*, *y*, and *z*.**

13.

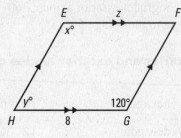

14.

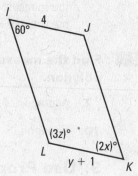

Find the indicated measure in ▱*MNOP*.

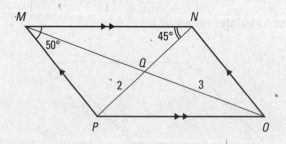

15. *MQ*	**16.** *MO*	**17.** *m∠PNO*
18. *m∠MPO*	**19.** *m∠NOP*	**20.** *PN*

BENCHMARK 4
A. Parallelograms

Name _____ Date _____

BENCHMARK 4
(Chapters 8 and 9)

4. Prove Quadrilaterals are Parallelograms

EXAMPLE

a. The diagram at right represents a baby gate which is secured to the floor and which has hinges at each corner. Explain why the top of the gate must always be parallel to the floor.

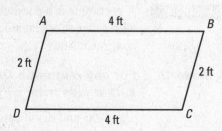

b. The glass in a four sided window is divided into triangles by wooden sticks whose lengths are related as shown in the diagram at the right. Explain how we know $\triangle ABE \cong \triangle CDE$.

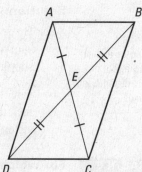

Solution:

a. The shape of the quadrilateral $ABCD$ changes as the hinges move around, but its side lengths do not change. Both pairs of opposite sides are congruent, so $ABCD$ is a parallelogram by Theorem 8.7. By the definition of parallelogram, $AB \parallel CD$, so the top of the gate must always be parallel to the floor.

You should memorize the results of Theorems 8.3 through 8.10.

b. According to the diagram, $\overline{AE} \cong \overline{EC}$ and $\overline{BE} \cong \overline{ED}$. Thus the diagonals of parallelogram $ABCD$ bisect each other. By Theorem 8.10, $ABCD$ is a parallelogram. Thus, $\overline{AB} \cong \overline{CD}$, by Theorem 8.3. We have $\triangle ABE \cong \triangle CDE$ by the SSS Congruence Postulate.

PRACTICE

State the theorem(s) you can use to show the quadrilateral is a parallelogram.

21.

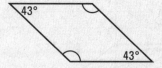

22.

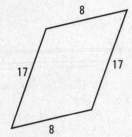

23.

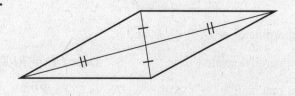

24.

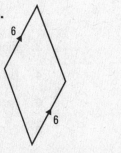

BENCHMARK 4
(Chapters 8 and 9)

5. Use Properties of Special Parallelograms

Vocabulary   A **rectangle** is a parallelogram with four right angles. A **rhombus** is a parallelogram with four congruent sides. A **square** is a parallelogram with four right angles and four congruent sides.

EXAMPLE   **For any rectangle *QRST*, decide whether the statement is *always* or *sometimes* true.**

   a. $\angle Q$ and $\angle S$ are supplementary.   **b.** $\overline{QR} \cong \overline{RS}$

Solution:

Remember:
Every square is a rectangle, but not every rectangle is a square!

   a. By definition, a rectangle is a parallelogram with four right angles. Thus the sum of any two angles is $90° + 90° = 180°$. So since every pair of angles is supplementary, $\angle Q$ and $\angle S$ are supplementary, and the statement is *always* true.

   b. If rectangle *QRST* is a square, then all sides are congruent so $\overline{QR} \cong \overline{RS}$. But if rectangle *QRST* is not a square, then consecutive sides are not congruent, so the statement is only *sometimes* true.

PRACTICE   **For which special parallelogram(s) *JKLM* is the statement always true? Explain your reasoning.**

   25. $\overline{JK} \cong \overline{KL}$ **26.** $\overrightarrow{JL}$ bisects $\angle MJK$ **27.** $\overline{JL} \cong \overline{KM}$

   28. $\overline{JL} \perp \overline{KM}, \overline{JL} \cong \overline{KM}$ **29.** $\angle K \cong \angle L$ **30.** $\angle K \cong \angle M$

Quiz

1. Three angles of a quadrilateral measure as follows: 157°, 38°, 98°. What is the measure of the fourth angle?

2. What is the measure of each exterior angle of an equilateral triangle?

Use the diagram.

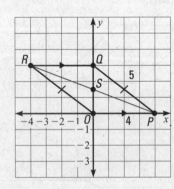

3. Find the coordinates of *O*, *P*, *Q*, *R*, and *S*.

4. Is *OPQR* a parallelogram?   5. Does *OQ = RP*?

6. Is *OPQR* a rectangle?   7. Is $\overline{OQ} \perp \overline{RP}$?

8. Is *OPQR* a rhombus?

BENCHMARK 4
A. Parallelograms

BENCHMARK 4
(Chapters 8 and 9)

B. Special Quadrilaterals

Just as there are special three-sided polygons, or triangles, which have certain properties, there are special four-sided polygons, or quadrilaterals, that we now characterize.

1. Prove a Quadrilateral is a Trapezoid

Vocabulary

A **trapezoid** is a quadrilateral with exactly one pair of parallel sides. These parallel sides are called **bases**. The endpoints of each base are the vertices for a pair of **base angles**. A trapezoid has two pairs of base angles. The nonparallel sides are the **legs** of the trapezoid.

EXAMPLE

Show that *ORST* is a trapezoid.

All pairs of vertical lines are parallel, even though they have undefined slope.

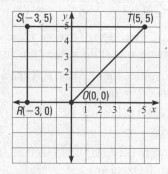

Solution:

Compare the slopes of opposite sides.

Slope of $\overline{RO} = \dfrac{0-0}{0-(-3)} = 0$ Slope of $\overline{ST} = \dfrac{5-5}{5-(-3)} = 0$

The slopes of $\overline{RO}$ and $\overline{ST}$ are the same so $\overline{RO} \parallel \overline{ST}$.

Slope of $\overline{TO} = \dfrac{5-0}{5-0} = \dfrac{5}{5} = 1$ Slope of $\overline{SR} = \dfrac{5-0}{-3-(-3)} = \dfrac{5}{0}$, which is undefined.

The slopes of $\overline{TO}$ and $\overline{SR}$ are not the same so $\overline{TO}$ is not parallel to $\overline{SR}$.

Because quadrilateral *ORST* has exactly one pair of parallel sides, it is a trapezoid.

PRACTICE

Points *A, B, C,* and *D* are the vertices of a quadrilateral. Determine whether *ABCD* is a trapezoid.

1. $A(2, 5), B(6, 5), C(10, -1), D(4, 2)$ 2. $A(-6, -1), B(1, 2), C(2, 0), D(-3, -3)$

3. $A(0, 3), B(4, 3), C(1, -1), D(-3, -2)$ 4. $A(-3, 6), B(-1, 4), C(1, -1), D(-3, 3)$

2. Use Properties of Isosceles Trapezoids

Vocabulary

A **trapezoid is isosceles** if its legs are congruent. The **midsegment of a trapezoid** is the line segment joining the midpoints of its legs.

BENCHMARK 4
B. Special Quadrilaterals

BENCHMARK 4
(Chapters 8 and 9)

EXAMPLE   The front of a park monument has a face in the shape of an isosceles trapezoid as depicted below. Find *m∠P*, *m∠R*, *m∠S*, and the length of the midsegment, *MN*. Must *MNRS* be an isosceles trapezoid as well?

Review methods for showing lines are parallel in Section 3.3.

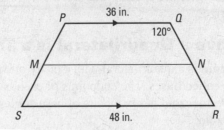

Solution:

Find *m∠P*. PQRS is an isosceles trapezoid, so ∠P and ∠Q are congruent base angles, and so *m∠P = m∠Q = 120°*.

Now find *m∠R*. Because ∠Q and ∠R are consecutive interior angles formed by $\overleftrightarrow{QR}$ intersecting two parallel lines, they are supplementary. So, *m∠R = 180° − 120° = 60°*.

To find *m∠S*, notice that ∠S and ∠R are a pair of base angles, so they are congruent, and *m∠S = m∠R = 60°*.

To find *MN*, use Theorem 8.17: $MN = \frac{1}{2}(PQ + RS) = \frac{1}{2}(36 + 48) = 42$. $\overline{MN}$ is 42 inches long.

Also by Theorem 8.17, $\overline{MN} \parallel \overline{RS}$ so that *MNRS* is a trapezoid. We have already observed that the base angles ∠R and ∠S are congruent, so by Theorem 8.15 it is an isosceles trapezoid.

PRACTICE   For each isosceles trapezoid *ABCD* shown, find: *m∠B*, *m∠C*, *m∠D*, the length of the diagonal *AC*, and the length of the midsegment $\overline{MN}$ (which is not drawn in the diagram).

5.
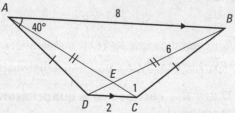

6.
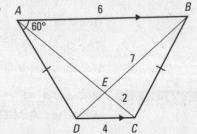

7.
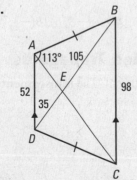

BENCHMARK 4
(Chapters 8 and 9)

3. Use Properties of Kites

Vocabulary

A **kite** is a quadrilateral that has two pairs of consecutive congruent sides, but opposite sides are not congruent.

EXAMPLE

Find $m\angle D$ in the kite shown below.

A quadrilateral is called a "kite" because it actually looks like a kite!

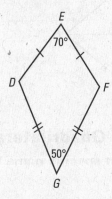

Solution:

By Theorem 8.19, *DEFG* has exactly one pair of congruent opposite angles. Because $m\angle E \neq m\angle G$ we must have that $m\angle D = m\angle F$. Write and solve an equation to find $m\angle D$.

$m\angle D + m\angle F + 70° + 50° = 360°$	**Corollary to Theorem 8.1**
$m\angle D + m\angle D + 70° + 50° = 360°$	**Substitute $m\angle D$ for $m\angle F$.**
$2(m\angle D) + 120° = 360°$	**Combine like terms.**
$m\angle D = 120°$	**Solve for $m\angle D$.**

PRACTICE

For the kite *HEFG* shown, find $m\angle H$.

8.

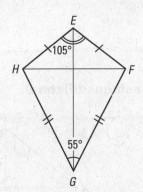

9.

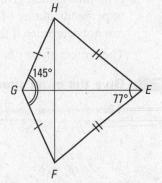

BENCHMARK 4
B. Special Quadrilaterals

BENCHMARK 4
(Chapters 8 and 9)

Use Theorem 8.18 and the Pythagorean Theorem to find the side lengths of the kite. Give your answer in simplest radical form.

10.
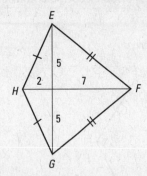

11.
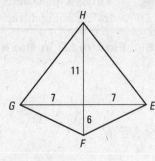

4. Identify a Quadrilateral

EXAMPLE   **What is the most specific name for quadrilateral *ABCD*?**

A. Parallelogram   **B.** Rhombus

Rely only on information that is marked on a diagram and what can be deduced from those markings.

C. Square   **D.** Rectangle

Solution:

The diagram shows $\angle B \cong \angle D$ and $\angle A \cong \angle C$. So, both pairs of opposite angles are congruent. By Theorem 8.8, *ABCD* is a parallelogram.

We notice too that the diagonals, $\overline{AC}$ and $\overline{BD}$ are perpendicular, so by Theorem 8.11, *ABCD* is a rhombus.

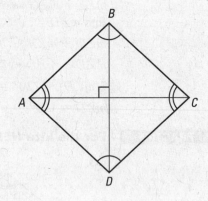

Squares are also rhombuses. However, there is no information given about the side lengths or perpendicularity of consecutive sides, so we can not determine if this rhombus is a square.

The correct answer is B.

PRACTICE   **Give the most specific name for each quadrilateral.**

12.
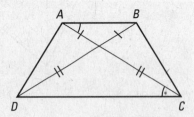

13.
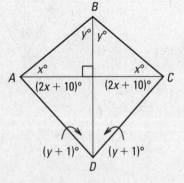

BENCHMARK 4
B. Special Quadrilaterals

BENCHMARK 4
(Chapters 8 and 9)

14.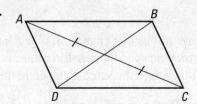

15.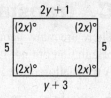

Quiz

Graph the trapezoid with vertices A(0, 0), B(0, 4), C(4, 6), and D(12, 6) and answer the questions that follow.

1. Which pair of sides are parallel and what are their slopes?

2. Is *ABCD* an isosceles trapezoid?

3. What is the length of the midsegment?

4. Solve for *x* in each figure.

a.

b.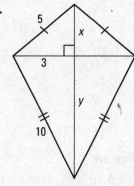

5. What is the most specific name for the quadrilateral shown below?

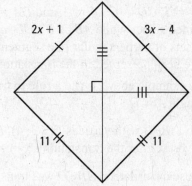

BENCHMARK 4
(Chapters 8 and 9)

C. Translations

There are many geometric transformations that change an object's position or orientation but not its shape or size. One specific transformation is called a *translation*. A translation moves every point of a figure the same distance in the same direction.

1. Write a Translation Rule and Verify Congruence

Vocabulary   A **translation** moves every point of a figure the same distance in the same direction. The new figure that has been transformed by a translation is called the **image**. The original figure is called the **preimage**. An **isometry** is a transformation that preserves length and angle measure.

EXAMPLE   **Use the diagram to write a rule for the translation of rectangle *ABCD* to rectangle *A'B'C'D'*. Then verify that the transformation is an isometry.**

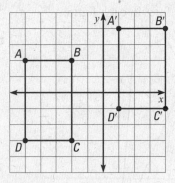

Solution:

To go from *A* to *A'*, move 6 units to the right and 2 units up. So a rule for the translation is $(x, y) \rightarrow (x + 6, y + 2)$.

Theorem 9.1, the Translation Theorem, states that every translation is an isometry.

To verify that the transformation is an isometry, find *AB*, *BC*, *CD*, and *DA* and compare these lengths with *A'B'*, *B'C'*, *C'D'*, and *D'A'*, respectively. Notice that $AB = A'B' = 3$, $BC = B'C' = 5$, $CD = C'D' = 3$, and $DA = D'A' = 5$. *DA, D'A', BC, and B'C'* all have undefined slopes while *AB, A'B', CD, and C'D'* all have slopes of 0. Therefore there are 4 sets of perpendicular line segments in each figure. The angles and side lengths have been preserved in the translation therefore making this an isometry.

PRACTICE

1. In the example above, write a rule to translate rectangle *A'B'C'D'* back to rectangle *ABCD*.

2. Graph △*EFG* with vertices $E(-3, 4)$, $F(1, 2)$ and $G(0, -3)$. Find the image of each vertex after the translation $(x, y) \rightarrow (x - 3, y + 2)$.

3. Suppose quadrilateral *ABCD* was translated to quadrilateral *A'B'C'D'*. Quadrilateral *ABCD* has coordinates $A(1, 3)$, $B(5, 4)$, $C(7, -5)$ and $D(0, -4)$ and quadrilateral *A'B'C'D'* has coordinates $A'(3, 0)$, $B'(7, 1)$, $C'(9, -8)$, and $D'(2, -7)$. Write a rule to translate quadrilateral *ABCD* to quadrilateral *A'B'C'D'*.

BENCHMARK 4
(Chapters 8 and 9)

2. Identify Vector Components

Vocabulary

A **vector** is a quantity that has both direction and magnitude, or size. A vector has a starting point called the **initial point** and an ending point called the **terminal point**. The **horizontal component** of the vector is the number of units left or right, *r*, from the initial point. The **vertical component** of the vector is the number of units up or down, *s*, from the initial point. The **component form** of a vector is $\langle r, s \rangle$.

EXAMPLE **Name the vector and write its component form.**

Recall that brackets are used to write the component form of the vector $\langle r, s \rangle$ and parentheses are used to write the coordinates of the point (p, q).

a.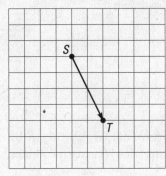

b.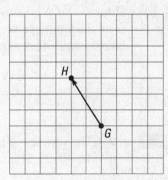

Solution:

a. The vector is $\overrightarrow{ST}$. From initial point *S* to terminal point *T*, you move 2 units to the right and 4 units down. So the component form is $\langle 2, -4 \rangle$.

b. The vector is $\overrightarrow{GH}$. From initial point *G* to terminal point *H*, you move 2 units to the left and 3 units up. So the component form is $\langle -2, 3 \rangle$.

PRACTICE **Name the vector and write its component form.**

4.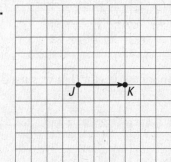

5.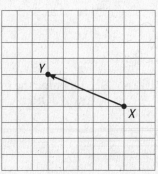

6.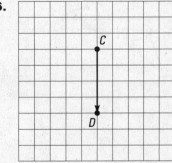

**BENCHMARK 4
C. Translations**

BENCHMARK 4

(Chapters 8 and 9)

3. Use a Vector to Translate a Figure

EXAMPLE

The vertices of △*LMN* are *L*(5, 4), *M*(−2, 3), and *N*(−4, −1). Translate △*LMN* using the vector ⟨3, −6⟩.

The first number in the component form of the vector gives how far to shift horizontally. The second number gives how far to shift vertically.

Solution:

First, graph △*LMN*. Use ⟨3, −6⟩ to move each vertex 3 units to the right and 6 units down. Label the image vertices. Draw △*L′M′N′*. Notice that the vectors drawn from the preimage vertices to the image vertices are parallel.

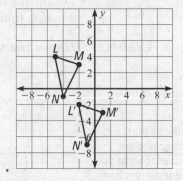

PRACTICE

7. The vertices of parallelogram *GRAM* are *G*(−7, −4), *R*(0, −4), *A*(3, 2), and *M*(−4, 2). Translate parallelogram *GRAM* using the vector ⟨−2, 4⟩.

8. △*X′Y′Z′* was translated using the following component vector ⟨−2, 3⟩. Find the original coordinates for the vertices of △*XYZ*.

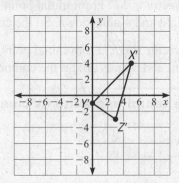

9. Examine the graph. Find the component vector that was used to translate △*ABC* to △*A′B′C′*.

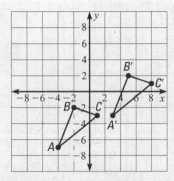

BENCHMARK 4
C. Translations

BENCHMARK 4
(Chapters 8 and 9)

4. Represent a Translation Using Matrices

Vocabulary

A **matrix** is a rectangular arrangement of numbers in rows and columns. Each number in the matrix is called an **element**. We add two matrices together to translate figures. One of the matrices is the **polygon matrix**, made up of vertices for the figure, and the other is the **translation matrix**, which includes elements that translate the *x* and *y* coordinates of the vertices. The resultant matrix is called the **image matrix**.

EXAMPLE

a. The matrix $\begin{bmatrix} -5 & -3 & 2 \\ 5 & 1 & 2 \end{bmatrix}$ represents $\triangle EFG$.

Find the image matrix that represents the translation of $\triangle EFG$ 2 units down and 4 units right.

Notice that the x-coordinates go in row one and the y-coordinates go in row two. Each column represents a different coordinate.

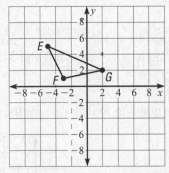

b. Examine the graph. What translation matrix was used to translate $\triangle PQR$?

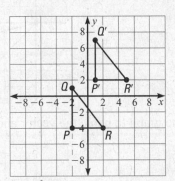

Solution:

a. Since we are moving 2 units down and 4 units right, the translation matrix is $\begin{bmatrix} 4 & 4 & 4 \\ -2 & -2 & -2 \end{bmatrix}$. Add the translation matrix to the polygon matrix. The resultant matrix is the new image matrix:

$$\begin{bmatrix} 4 & 4 & 4 \\ -2 & -2 & -2 \end{bmatrix} + \begin{bmatrix} -5 & -3 & 2 \\ 5 & 1 & 2 \end{bmatrix} = \begin{bmatrix} -1 & 1 & 6 \\ 3 & -1 & 0 \end{bmatrix}$$

      Translation Matrix   **Polygon Matrix**   **Image Matrix**

b. Since each vertex of the triangle was moved right 3 units and up 6 units, the translation matrix is $\begin{bmatrix} 3 & 3 & 3 \\ 6 & 6 & 6 \end{bmatrix}$.

PRACTICE

10. The matrix $\begin{bmatrix} 0 & 4 & 4 & 0 \\ 0 & 0 & -2 & -2 \end{bmatrix}$ represents rectangle *ABCD*. Find the image that represents the translation of rectangle *ABCD* 6 units up and 5 units left.

BENCHMARK 4
C. Translations

BENCHMARK 4
(Chapters 8 and 9)

11. Examine the graph. What translation matrix was used to translate △*DEF*?

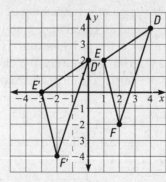

12. The matrix $\begin{bmatrix} 2 & 4 \\ -4 & 1 \end{bmatrix}$ represents $\overline{AB}$. Find the image matrix that represents the translation of $\overline{AB}$ 6 units left and 3 units down. Then graph $\overline{AB}$ and its image.

Quiz

1. Use the graph to write a rule for the translation of △*HIJ* to △*H'I'J'*.

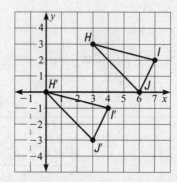

2. Use the graph to name the vector and write its component form.

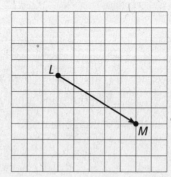

BENCHMARK 4
(Chapters 8 and 9)

3. The vertices of $\triangle RST$ are $R(2, 4)$, $S(3, -3)$, and $T(-2, -4)$. Translate $\triangle RST$ using the vector $\langle -4, 3 \rangle$.

4. Use the translation $(x, y) \rightarrow (x - 4, y + 1)$.

   a. What is the image of $(-2, 4)$?

   b. What is the preimage of $(-5, -2)$?

5. Use the graph. Find the image matrix that represents the translation of $\triangle JKL$ 4 units left and 3 units down. List the translation matrix, polygon matrix, and image matrix.

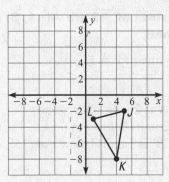

BENCHMARK 4
(Chapters 8 and 9)

D. Reflections, Rotations, and Dilations

There are many geometric transformations that change an object's position or orientation but not its shape or size. In this section you will perform three types of transformations called reflections, rotations, and dilations.

1. Graph a Reflection

Vocabulary

A **reflection** is a transformation that uses a line like a mirror to reflect an image. The mirror line is called the **line of reflection**.

EXAMPLE **The endpoints of $\overline{AB}$ are $A(-4, 3)$ and $B(2, 6)$. Graph the reflection of $\overline{AB}$ as described.**

Coordinate Rules
for Reflections:
If (a, b) is reflected
in the:
x-axis:
$(a, b) \rightarrow (a, -b)$
y-axis:
$(a, b) \rightarrow (-a, b)$
$y = x$:
$(a, b) \rightarrow (b, a)$
$y = -x$:
$(a, b) \rightarrow (-b, -a)$

a. In the line $r : y = 1$ **b.** In the line $\ell : x = -1$

Solution:

a. Point A is 2 units above r, so
A' is 2 units below r at $(-4, -1)$.
Also, B' is 5 units below r at $(2, -4)$.

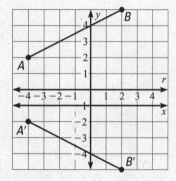

b. Point A is 3 units left of ℓ, so
A' is 3 units right of ℓ at $(2, 3)$.
Also, B' is 3 units left of ℓ at $(-4, 6)$.

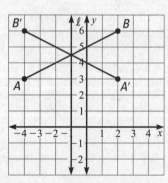

PRACTICE **Graph $\overline{MN}$ with endpoints $M(4, -3)$ and $N(2, 4)$.**

  1. Find the endpoints of $\overline{M'N'}$ reflected in line $s : y = -2$.

  2. Find the endpoints of $\overline{M''N''}$ reflected in the line $t : x = 1$.

EXAMPLE **The endpoints of $\overline{TH}$ are $T(-2, 2)$ and $H(0, 3)$.**

  a. Reflect the segment in the line $y = x$. Graph the segment and its image.

  b. Reflect the segment in the line $y = -x$. Graph the segment and its image.

BENCHMARK 4
D. Transformations

BENCHMARK 4
(Chapters 8 and 9)

Solution:

a. The slope of $y = x$ is 1. The segment from T to its image, $\overline{TT'}$, is perpendicular to the line of reflection $y = x$, so the slope of $\overline{TT'}$ will be -1 (because $1(-1) = -1$). From T, move 2 units right and 2 units down to $y = x$. From that point move 2 units right and 2 units down to locate $T'(2, -2)$. The slope of $\overline{HH'}$ will also be -1. From H, move 1.5 units right and 1.5 units down to $y = x$. Then move 1.5 units right and 1.5 units down to $H'(3, 0)$.

b. Use the coordinate rule for reflecting in $y = -x$.

$$(a, b) \rightarrow (-b, -a)$$
$$T(-2, 2) \rightarrow T'(-2, 2)$$
$$H(0, 3) \rightarrow H'(-3, 0)$$

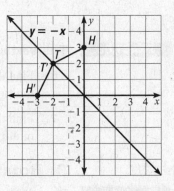

PRACTICE   Graph $\overline{JK}$ with endpoints $J(-2, -5)$ and $K(5, 1)$.

3. Find the endpoints of $\overline{J'K'}$ reflected in line $y = x$.

4. Verify that $\overline{JJ'}$ is perpendicular to $y = x$.

5. Find the endpoints of $\overline{J''K''}$ reflected in the line $y = -x$.

2. Use Matrix Multiplication to Reflect a Polygon

EXAMPLE   The vertices of $\triangle PQR$ are $P(-3, 2)$, $Q(2, 2)$, and $R(2, -1)$. Find the reflection of $\triangle PQR$ in the x-axis using matrix multiplication. Graph $\triangle PQR$ and its image.

Solution:

Step 1: Multiply the polygon matrix by the matrix for a reflection in the x-axis.

$$\begin{bmatrix} 1 & 0 \\ 0 & -1 \end{bmatrix}\begin{bmatrix} -3 & 2 & 2 \\ 2 & 2 & -1 \end{bmatrix} = \begin{bmatrix} 1(-3) + 0(2) & 1(2) + 0(2) & 1(2) + 0(2) \\ 0(-3) + -1(2) & 0(2) + -1(2) & 0(2) + -1(-1) \end{bmatrix}$$

$$= \begin{bmatrix} -3 & 2 & 2 \\ -2 & -2 & 1 \end{bmatrix}. \text{ This is the image matrix.}$$

BENCHMARK 4
(Chapters 8 and 9)

Step 2: Graph $\triangle PQR$ and $\triangle P'Q'R'$.

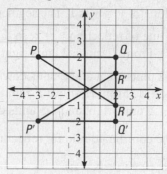

The vertices of $\triangle FED$ are $F(-4, -2)$, $E(1, 2)$, and $D(3, -3)$.

6. Find the vertices of the image reflected over the *x*-axis using matrix multiplication.

7. Find the vertices of the image reflected over the *y*-axis using matrix multiplication.

3. Rotate a Figure

Vocabulary

Rays drawn from the center of rotation to a point and its image form the **angle of rotation**.

EXAMPLE

Graph $\triangle XYZ$ with vertices $X(-4, -3)$, $Y(-1, -1)$, and $Z(-1, -4)$. Rotate $\triangle XYZ$ 180° about the origin.

Solution:

Coordinate Rules for Rotations about the Origin:
If (a, b) is rotated counterclockwise about the origin, then for a rotation of 90°,
$(a, b) \rightarrow (-b, a)$
For a rotation of 180°,
$(a, b) \rightarrow (-a, -b)$
For a rotation of 270°,
$(a, b) \rightarrow (b, -a)$

Graph $\triangle XYZ$. Use the coordinate rule for a 180° rotation to find the images of the vertices:

$(a, b) \rightarrow (-a, -b)$:

$X(-4, -3) \rightarrow X'(4, 3)$

$Y(-1, -1) \rightarrow Y'(1, 1)$

$Z(-1, -4) \rightarrow Z'(1, 4)$

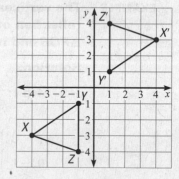

Graph $\triangle STU$ with vertices $S(-5, 0)$, $T(-2, 4)$, and $U(1, -2)$ and its image after each rotation.

8. Rotate the triangle 90° about the origin.

9. Rotate the triangle 180° about the origin.

10. Rotate the triangle 270° about the origin.

BENCHMARK 4
(Chapters 8 and 9)

EXAMPLE   Quadrilateral *ABCD* has vertices *A*(−5, −1), *B*(−3, 2), *C*(0, −2) and *D*(−1, −4). Use matrix multiplication to find the image matrix for a 270° rotation of *ABCD* about the origin. Graph *ABCD* and its image.

Solution:

Step 1: Write the polygon matrix. $\begin{bmatrix} -5 & -3 & 0 & -1 \\ -1 & 2 & -2 & -4 \end{bmatrix}$.

Step 2: Multiply by the matrix for a 270° rotation:

$$\begin{bmatrix} 0 & 1 \\ -1 & 0 \end{bmatrix} \begin{bmatrix} -5 & -3 & 0 & -1 \\ -1 & 2 & -2 & -4 \end{bmatrix} = \begin{bmatrix} -1 & 2 & -2 & -4 \\ 5 & 3 & 0 & 1 \end{bmatrix}.$$

Step 3: Graph the preimage *ABCD* and image *A′B′C′D′*.

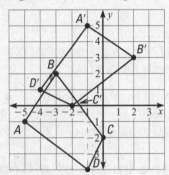

PRACTICE   Graph △*TUV* with vertices *T*(3, 2), *U*(5, 5), and *V*(6, 1) and its image after each rotation.

11. Rotate the triangle 90° about the origin using matrices.

12. Rotate the triangle 270° about the origin using matrices.

13. Rotate the triangle 360° about the origin using matrices.

4. Use Scalar Multiplication in a Dilation

Vocabulary   A **dilation** is a transformation in which the original figure and its image are similar. A **reduction** to the figure occurs when the scale factor, *k*, is between 0 and 1. An **enlargement** to the figure occurs when the scale factor, *k*, is greater than 1.

EXAMPLE   The vertices of △*CBA* are *C*(−6, 1), *B*(2, 3), and *A*(1, −4). Find the image of △*CBA* after the given composition.

A reduction can also be called a contraction.

Translation: $(x, y) \rightarrow (x - 2, y + 3)$

Dilation: centered at origin with a scale factor of $\frac{1}{2}$.

Solution:

Step 1: Graph the preimage △*CBA* in the coordinate plane.

Step 2: Translate △*CBA* 2 units to the left and 3 units up. Graph the image △*C′B′A′*.

BENCHMARK 4
(Chapters 8 and 9)

Step 3: Dilate $\triangle C'B'A'$ using the origin as the center and a

scale factor of $\frac{1}{2}$ to find $\triangle C''B''A''$.

$$\frac{1}{2}\begin{bmatrix} -8 & 0 & -1 \\ 4 & 6 & -1 \end{bmatrix} = \begin{bmatrix} -4 & 0 & -\frac{1}{2} \\ 2 & 3 & -\frac{1}{2} \end{bmatrix}$$

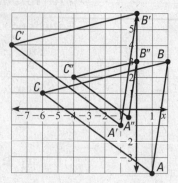

PRACTICE

14. The vertices of $\triangle MNO$ are $M(6, 5)$, $N(3, 2)$, and $O(1, 4)$. Use scalar multiplication to find the vertices of $\triangle M'N'O'$ after a dilation with its center at the origin and a scale factor of 3.

15. A segment has the endpoints $B(-4, 2)$ and $C(3, -3)$. Find the endpoints of the image of $\overline{BC}$ after a 180° rotation about the origin followed by a dilation with its center at the origin and a scale factor of 2.

5. Find the Image of a Composition

Vocabulary

A **glide reflection** is a transformation in which every point in the figure is translated by some rule and then reflected in a given line.

EXAMPLE

The vertices of $\triangle JKL$ are $J(-6, -2)$, $K(-4, -4)$, and $L(-1, -2)$.

Generally speaking, the order in which transformations are composed will make a difference.

a. Find the image of $\triangle JKL$ after the glide reflection:

Translation: $(x, y) \rightarrow (x + 6, y + 5)$

Reflection: in the y-axis

b. Find the image of $\triangle JKL$ after the composition:

Reflection: in the x-axis

Rotation: 180° about the origin.

Solution:

a. Begin by graphing $\triangle JKL$. Then graph $\triangle J'K'L'$ after a translation 6 units right and 5 units up. Finally, graph $\triangle J''K''L''$ after a reflection in the y-axis.

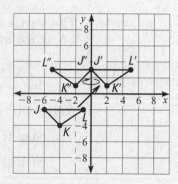

BENCHMARK 4
(Chapters 8 and 9)

b. Begin by graphing △*JKL*. Then graph
△*J'K'L'* after a reflection in the *x*-axis
using $(a, b) \rightarrow (a, -b)$. Finally, graph
△*J"K"L"* after a rotation of 180° about
the origin using $(a, b) \rightarrow (-a, -b)$.

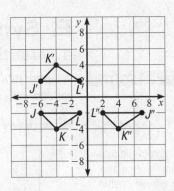

PRACTICE   **The vertices of △*ABC* are *A*(1, −3), *B*(3, −1), and *C*(5, −4).**

16. Find the image of △*ABC* after the glide reflection:

Translation: $(x, y) \rightarrow (x - 2, y + 5)$
Reflection: in the *x*-axis

17. Find the image of △*ABC* after the composition:

Reflection: in the *y*-axis
Rotation: −90° about the origin

The vertices of △*DEF* are *D*(−2, 1), *E*(−3, 4), and *F*(−1, 5).

18. Find the image of △*DEF* after the composition:

Rotation: 180° about the origin
Translation: $(x, y) \rightarrow (x - 4, y - 2)$

19. Find the image of △*ABC* after the glide reflection:

Translation: $(x, y) \rightarrow (x + 4, y - 5)$
Reflection: in the *y*-axis

Quiz

**The endpoints of $\overline{RS}$ are *R*(−5, −2) and *S*(−3, −4). Find the endpoints of
the segment after a reflection about the given line.**

1. Line *m* : $y = 2$ **2.** The line $y = -x$.

Find the coordinates of the image of *G*(−4, 2) after the given rotation.

3. Rotate 270° about the origin.   **4.** Rotate 90° about the origin.

5. The vertices of △*EFG* are *E*(−4, −5), *F*(−1, 4), and *G*(−2, −3). Find the
image of △*EFG* after the given composition.

Translation: $(x, y) \rightarrow (x + 4, y + 2)$
Dilation: centered at origin with a scale factor of 2.

6. The endpoints of $\overline{DE}$ are *D*(6, −2), and *E*(4, −5). Find the image of $\overline{DE}$ after
the given glide reflection.

Translation: $(x, y) \rightarrow (x - 8, y + 7)$
Reflection: in the *x*-axis

BENCHMARK 4
D. Transformations

BENCHMARK 4
(Chapters 8 and 9)

E. Symmetry
1. Identify Lines of Symmetry

Vocabulary A figure in a plane has **line symmetry** if the figure can be mapped onto itself by a reflection in a line. This line is called the **line of symmetry**.

EXAMPLE **How many lines of symmetry does each figure have?**

If you could fold the figure along a crease so that each of the two halves formed line up exactly, the figure has line symmetry and the crease is the line of symmetry.

a.   b.  c.   d.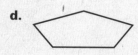

Solution:

a. Four lines of symmetry.   **b.** One line of symmetry.

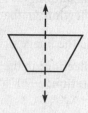

c. Three lines of symmetry.   **d.** One line of symmetry.

PRACTICE **How many lines of symmetry does the object appear to have?**

1. 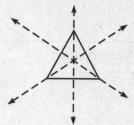   2.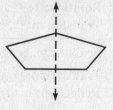

3.    4.

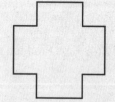   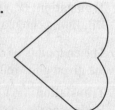

5. Draw a triangle with no lines of symmetry.

Name _____ Date _____

BENCHMARK 4
(Chapters 8 and 9)

2. Identify Rotational Symmetry

Vocabulary A figure in a plane has **rotational symmetry** if the figure can be mapped onto itself by a rotation of 180° or less about the center of the figure. This point is called the **center of symmetry**.

EXAMPLE **Does the figure have rotational symmetry? If so, describe any rotations that map the figure onto itself.**

Every rotation of a circle about its center maps a circle onto itself.

a. Regular Pentagon

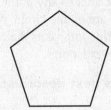

b. Equilateral Triangle

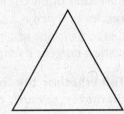

Solution:

   a. Yes. Any rotation, clockwise or counterclockwise, which is an integer multiple of 72° maps the image onto itself.

   b. Yes. Any rotation, clockwise or counterclockwise, which is an integer multiple of 60° maps the image onto itself.

PRACTICE **Does the figure have rotational symmetry? If so, describe any rotations that map the figure onto itself.**

6.

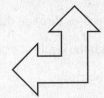

7.

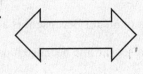

8.

Quiz

Draw a figure for the description, if possible.

   1. A triangle with one line of symmetry.

   2. A quadrilateral with two lines of symmetry.

   3. True or false? A square has 90° rotational symmetry.

   4. Determine whether or not the figure below has rotational symmetry.

BENCHMARK 5
(Chapters 10 and 11)

A. Circles and Special Segments and Lines

In this section you will learn about circles. You will identify and use parts of circles to solve problems.

1. Identify Special Segments and Lines

Vocabulary   A **circle** is a set of all points in a plane that are equidistant from a given point called the **center** of the circle. The segment from the center to any point on the circle is a **radius**. A **chord** is a segment whose endpoints are on the circle. A **diameter** is a chord that contains the center of the circle. A **secant line** intersects the circle at two points while a **tangent line** intersects the circle at only one point.

EXAMPLE   **Tell whether the line, ray, or segment is best described as radius, chord, diameter, secant, or tangent of ⊙D.**

a. $\overline{BH}$ **b.** $\overleftrightarrow{GC}$ **c.** $\overline{BA}$ **d.** $\overline{CE}$

A line segment is tangent to a circle if it intersects the circle at only one point and is contained in a tangent line.

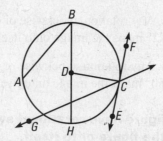

Solution:

a. $\overline{BH}$ is a diameter because it is a chord that passes through the center.

b. $\overleftrightarrow{GC}$ is a secant line because it passes through the circle at exactly two points.

c. $\overline{BA}$ is a chord because it has endpoints on the circle.

d. $\overline{CE}$ is a tangent line because it intersects the circle at only one point.

PRACTICE   **Use the diagram to name the following.**

1. Center

2. Radius

3. Diameter

4. Chord that is not a diameter.

5. Ray that is a secant.

6. Tangent line

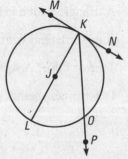

BENCHMARK 5
(Chapters 10 and 11)

2. Use Properties of Tangents

EXAMPLE

In the diagram, *F* is the point of tangency. Find the length of the radius of the circle. *EG* = 26 cm, *GF* = 24 cm.

When the radius of a circle intersects a tangent line at the point of tangency, the lines form a right angle.

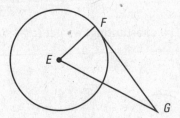

Solution:

$\overline{EF} \perp \overline{FG}$, so $\triangle EFG$ is a right triangle. By the Pythagorean Theorem, $EF^2 + FG^2 = EG^2$, so substitute to get $EF^2 + 24^2 = 26^2$. Thus, $EF^2 = 26^2 - 24^2 = 100$. Therefore, $EF = 10$. Since $\overline{EF}$ is the radius, the radius of the circle is 10 cm.

PRACTICE

7. Find the length, *r*, of the radius of the circle.

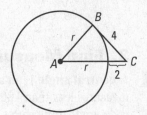

8. Is $\overline{JK} \perp \overline{KL}$?

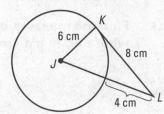

9. Given *AC* = 20, *CD* = 14, find *ED*. Round to nearest tenth.

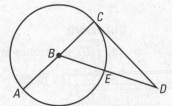

EXAMPLE

In the diagram, $\overline{LB}$ and $\overline{LC}$ are tangent lines of $\odot E$. Find the value of *x* and the lengths of $\overline{LB}$ and $\overline{LC}$.

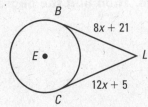

BENCHMARK 5
(Chapters 10 and 11)

Solution:

$LB = LC$ because tangent segments from the same point are congruent.

$$12x + 5 = 8x + 21$$
$$x = 4$$

Therefore, by substituting, we get $LB = LC = 53$.

PRACTICE   **10.** Find x.

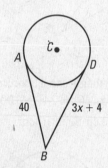

40     $3x + 4$

11. Find x.

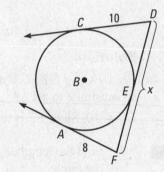

10   8

3. Find Measures of Arcs

Vocabulary   A **central angle** is an angle whose vertex is the center of the circle. A **minor arc** measures less than 180°. A **major arc** measures greater than 180°. A **semicircle** is an arc that measures exactly 180°.

EXAMPLE   **Find the measure of each arc of ⊙A, where $\overline{BC}$ is a diameter.**

The measure of an arc is the same as the central angle that determines it.

  a. $\overparen{BD}$

  b. $\overparen{DC}$

  c. $\overparen{CBD}$

  d. $\overparen{BDC}$

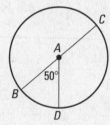

Solution:

  a. $\overparen{BD}$ is a minor arc, so $m\overparen{BD} = m\angle BAD = 50°$.

  b. $\overparen{DC}$ is a minor arc, so $m\overparen{DC} = m\angle DAC = 180 - 50 = 130°$.

  c. $\overparen{CBD}$ is a major arc, so $m\overparen{CBD} = 360 - 130 = 230°$.

  d. $\overparen{BDC}$ is a semicircle so $m\overparen{BDC} = 180°$.

PRACTICE   **Identify each arc as a *minor arc, major arc*, or *semicircle*. Then find the degree measure of the arc.**

  12. $\overparen{BCE}$

  13. $\overparen{AE}$

  14. $\overparen{BAC}$

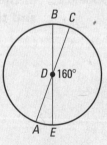

BENCHMARK 5
(Chapters 10 and 11)

EXAMPLE **Find the measure of the arc of ⊙C using the Arc Addition Postulate.**

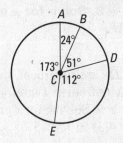

a. $\overset{\frown}{AD}$

b. $\overset{\frown}{ADE}$

Solution:

a. $m\overset{\frown}{AD} = m\overset{\frown}{AB} + m\overset{\frown}{BD} = 75°$

b. $m\overset{\frown}{ADE} = m\overset{\frown}{AD} + m\overset{\frown}{DE} = 187°$

PRACTICE **Use the Angle Addition Postulate to find the degree measures of the following arcs.**

15. $\overset{\frown}{BD}$

16. $\overset{\frown}{BED}$

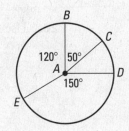

4. Use Congruent Chords

EXAMPLE **In ⊙I, $\overline{EF} \cong \overline{FG}$ and $m\overset{\frown}{EHG} = 200°$. Find $m\overset{\frown}{EF}$.**

Two chords of a circle are congruent if and only if the arcs they subtend have the same measure.

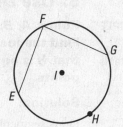

Solution:

$m\overset{\frown}{EF} + m\overset{\frown}{FG} + m\overset{\frown}{EHG} = 360°$

$m\overset{\frown}{EF} + m\overset{\frown}{FG} + 200° = 360°$ **Substitute.**

$m\overset{\frown}{EF} + m\overset{\frown}{FG} = 160°$ **Subtract.**

Since $\overline{EF} \cong \overline{FG}$, we know by Theorem 10.3 that

$m\overset{\frown}{EF} = m\overset{\frown}{FG}$, so $2m\overset{\frown}{EF} = 160°$ or

$m\overset{\frown}{EF} = 160° \div 2 = 80°$.

PRACTICE **Use the diagram of ⊙E to find the measure of the arc.**

17. $\overset{\frown}{AC}$

18. $\overset{\frown}{ACB}$

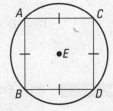

BENCHMARK 5
(Chapters 10 and 11)

EXAMPLE   In the diagram of ⊙A, $\overline{BC} \cong \overline{DE}$ and AF = 4x + 3 and AG = 2x + 9. Solve for x and find the measure of AF.

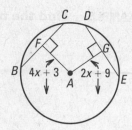

Solution:

Chords $\overline{BC}$ and $\overline{DE}$ are congruent, so by Theorem 10.6 they are equidistant from A. Therefore, AF = AG and so 4x + 3 = 2x + 9. Solving for x gives x = 3. So, AF = 4x + 3 = 4(3) + 3 = 15.

PRACTICE   **19.** Use ⊙C, and the information given to find the value of x.

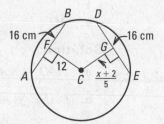

20. Use ⊙S, and the information given to find SY.

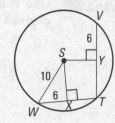

5. Use Diameters

EXAMPLE   Points **A, B,** and **C** are shown. Find the location of point **H** so that **H** is equidistant to all three points.

Every diameter is a chord, but not every chord is a diameter.

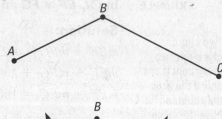

Solution:

Draw segments $\overline{AB}$ and $\overline{BC}$. Then draw the perpendicular bisectors of $\overline{AB}$ and $\overline{BC}$. By Theorem 10.4, these are diameters of the circle containing A, B, and C. The point where the two bisectors intersect is the center of this circle, so it is equidistant to each point.

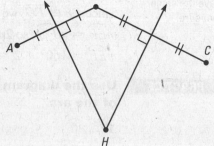

PRACTICE   **21.** Points J, K, and L are shown. Find the location of point M, so that M is equidistant to all three points.

BENCHMARK 5
(Chapters 10 and 11)

EXAMPLE　In the diagram of $\odot F$, $EG = 34$ and $IJ = 15$.

    a. Find the length of $\overline{HI}$.

    b. Find the length of $\overline{JF}$.

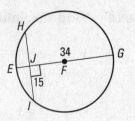

Solution:

    a. Diameter $\overline{EG}$ is perpendicular to $\overline{HI}$. So by, Theorem 10.5, $\overline{EG}$ bisects $\overline{HI}$, and $HJ = JI$. Therefore, $HI = 2(IJ) = 2(15) = 30$.

    b. Draw a line segment with endpoints $\overline{HF}$. Because $\overline{HF}$ is a radius of the circle, the length of $\overline{HF}$ is $\frac{1}{2} EG = 17$. Using the Pythagorean Theorem, we see that $HJ^2 + JF^2 = HF^2$, so we get $15^2 + JF^2 = 17^2$. Solving for JF gives $JF^2 = 17^2 - 15^2 = 64$. Therefore, $JF = 8$.

PRACTICE　Use the diagram for Exercises 22 and 23.

  22. Find the length of $\overline{ON}$.

  23. Find the length of $\overline{PO}$. Round to two decimal places.

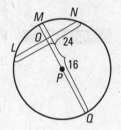

6. Find Segment Lengths in Circles

Vocabulary　When two chords intersect in the interior of a circle, each chord is divided into two segments that are called **segments of the chord**.

EXAMPLE

Theorem 10.14 states that if two chords intersect in the interior of a circle, then the product of the lengths of the segments of one chord is equal to the product of the lengths of the segments of the other chord.

Find the value of x.

Solution:

$EI \cdot IG = FI \cdot IH$, so $5x = (3)(10) = 30$.

Solve for x to get $x = 6$.

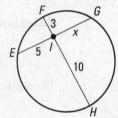

PRACTICE　Find the value of **x**.

24.
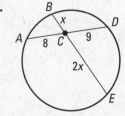

25.
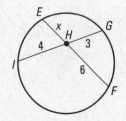

BENCHMARK 5
(Chapters 10 and 11)

EXAMPLE   **Find the value of x.**

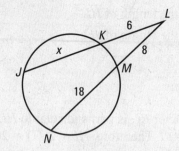

Solution:

$LK \cdot LJ = LM \cdot LN$ Use Theorem 10.15.

$6(6 + x) = 8(8 + 18)$ Substitute.

$36 + 6x = 208$ Simplify.

Solve for x to get $x = \dfrac{86}{3}$.

PRACTICE   **Find the value of x.**

26.

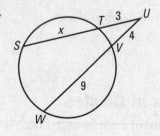

27.

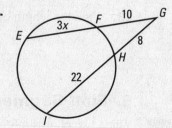

EXAMPLE   **In the diagram, find the value of x.**

Solution:

$x \cdot x = 3(3 + 9)$ Use Theorem 10.16.

$x^2 = 36$

Therefore, $x = 6$.

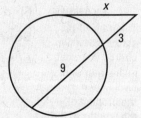

PRACTICE   **Find the value of x.**

28.

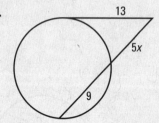

29.

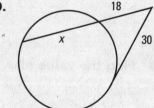

Geometry
Benchmark 5 Chapters 10 and 11

118

BENCHMARK 5

(Chapters 10 and 11)

Quiz

Use the diagram of ⊙C for Exercises 1–3.

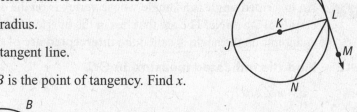

1. Name a chord that is not a diameter.

2. Name a radius.

3. Name a tangent line.

4. In ⊙A, B is the point of tangency. Find x.

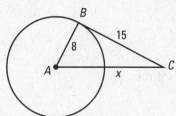

Use the diagram of ⊙B for Exercises 5 and 6. $\overline{AD}$ and $\overline{EC}$ are diameters.

5. Find $m\angle ABC$.

6. Find $m\angle ADE$.

7. Find $m\overset{\frown}{ADE}$.

8. Find $m\overset{\frown}{CD}$.

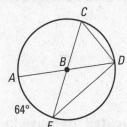

Use the diagram of ⊙E for Exercises 9 and 10. $\overline{BF}$ is a diameter. AD = 12 and BF = 20.

9. Find AC.

10. Find BC.

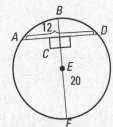

In Exercises 11–13, find the value of x.

11.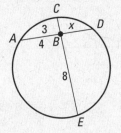

12.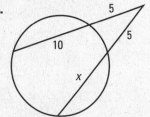

13.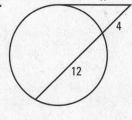

BENCHMARK 5
(Chapters 10 and 11)

B. Angle Relationships in Circles

1. Use Inscribed Angles and Intercepted Arcs

Vocabulary

An **inscribed angle** is an angle whose vertex is on the circle and whose sides contain chords of the circle. The arc that lies in the interior of an inscribed angle and has endpoints on the angle is called the **intercepted arc** of the angle.

EXAMPLE

Two chords of a circle with a common endpoint determine an inscribed angle.

Find the indicated measure in $\odot C$.

a. $m\angle ABD$

b. $m\overset{\frown}{BE}$

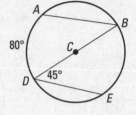

Solution:

a. $m\angle ABD = \frac{1}{2}\, m\overset{\frown}{AD} = \frac{1}{2}80° = 40°$

b. $m\overset{\frown}{BE} = 2m\angle BDE = 2(45°) = 90°$

PRACTICE

Find the indicated measures in $\odot E$.

1. $m\angle DCB$

2. $m\overset{\frown}{AC}$

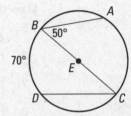

EXAMPLE

Find the indicated measure in $\odot F$.

a. $m\overset{\frown}{AE}$

b. $m\angle ACE$

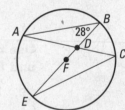

Solution:

a. $m\overset{\frown}{AE} = 2m\angle ABE = 56°$

b. $m\angle ACE = m\angle ABE = 28°$ by Theorem 10.8

PRACTICE

Find the indicated measures in $\odot J$.

3. $m\angle FIH$

4. $m\overset{\frown}{FH}$

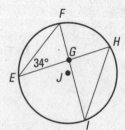

BENCHMARK 5
(Chapters 10 and 11)

2. Use Inscribed Quadrilaterals

Vocabulary   A polygon is an **inscribed polygon** if all of its vertices lie on a circle.

EXAMPLE   **Find the values of *x* and *y*.**

Solution:

Every angle of an inscribed polygon is an inscribed angle.

EFGH is inscribed in a circle, so opposite angles are supplementary:

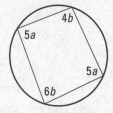

$m\angle HEF + m\angle HGF = 180°$	Use Theorem 10.10.
$85 + y = 180$	Substitute.
$y = 95$	Solve for *y*.
$m\angle EHF + m\angle EFG = 180°$	Use Theorem 10.10.
$90 + x = 180$	Substitute.
$x = 90$	Solve for *x*.

PRACTICE

5. Find the value of *a*.

6. Find the value of *b*.

3. Other Angle Relationships in Circles

EXAMPLE   **Line *n* is tangent to the circle. Find the measure of the angle or arc.**

If a radius and a tangent line of a circle intersect, then they are perpendicular.

a. $\angle 1$

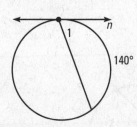

b. $\widehat{ABC}$

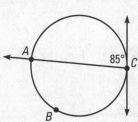

Solution:

a. $m\angle 1 = \frac{1}{2}(140) = 70°$

b. $m\angle ACB = 180 - 85 = 95°$
$m\widehat{ABC} = 2(95) = 190°$

PRACTICE

7. Find $m\angle 1$.

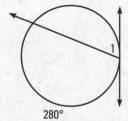

8. Find $m\widehat{BCA}$.

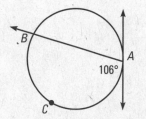

BENCHMARK 5
(Chapters 10 and 11)

EXAMPLE   **Find the value of x.**

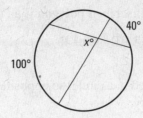

Solution:

$$x° = \frac{1}{2}(40° + 100°) = 70°$$

PRACTICE   **9.** Find the value of *x*.   **10.** Find the value of *y*.

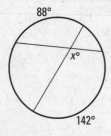   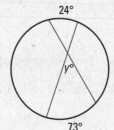

EXAMPLE   **Find the value of x.**

Solution:

$$x° = \frac{1}{2}(84° - 28°) = 28°$$

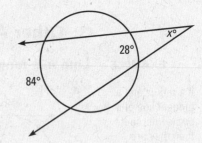

PRACTICE   **11.** Find the value of *x*.

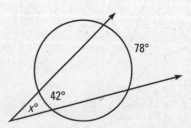

12. Find the value of *y*.

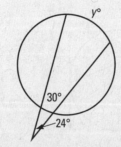

BENCHMARK 5
(Chapters 10 and 11)

4. Write the Standard Equation of a Circle

Vocabulary The **standard equation of a circle** with center (h, k) and radius r is:

$(x - h)^2 + (y - k)^2 = r^2$.

EXAMPLE **Write the standard equation of the circle with center $(-2, 3)$ and radius 7.**

Solution:

$(x - h)^2 + (y - k)^2 = r^2$	Standard equation of a circle.
$(x - (-2))^2 + (y - 3)^2 = 7^2$	Substitute.
$(x + 2)^2 + (y - 3)^2 = 49$	Simplify.

PRACTICE **Write the standard equation of a circle with the given center and radius.**

13. Center $(-1, 2)$, radius 4   **14.** Center $(4, -2)$, radius 6

EXAMPLE **The point (5, 5) is on a circle with center (2, 2). Write the standard equation of the circle.**

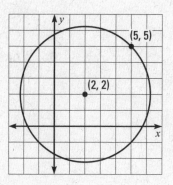

Solution:

To write the standard equation, you need to know the values of h, k, and r. To find r, find the distance between the center and the point $(5, 5)$ on the circle.

$r = \sqrt{(5 - 2)^2 + (5 - 2)^2} = \sqrt{18}$ **Distance Formula**

Therefore the standard form of the equation is $(x - 2)^2 + (y - 2)^2 = 18$.

PRACTICE **15.** The point $(-2, 0)$ is on a circle whose center is $(0, 0)$. Write the standard equation of the circle.

16. The point $(-3, -4)$ is on a circle whose center is $(1, 2)$. Write the standard equation of the circle.

Quiz

Find the indicated measures in $\odot T$.

1. $m\angle ABC$

2. $m\angle 1$

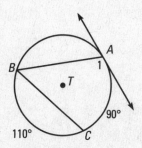

BENCHMARK 5
(Chapters 10 and 11)

For Exercises 3–5, find the value of *x*.

3.

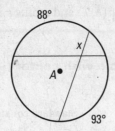

4.

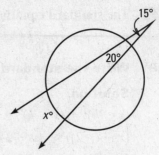

5.

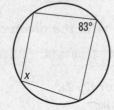

6. Write the standard equation of a circle with center $(-6, 2)$ and diameter 12.

BENCHMARK 5
(Chapters 10 and 11)

C. Circumference and Area of Circles

Throughout this section, you should use the π key on your calculator, then round to the hundredths place unless instructed otherwise.

1. Find a Circumference

Vocabulary

The **circumference** of a circle is the distance around the circle. For all circles, the ratio of the circumference to the diameter is the constant value π.

EXAMPLE

Find the indicated measure.

For a fascinating introduction to the number π, read "A History of π" by Petr Beckmann.

a. The circumference of a circle with radius 19 inches.

b. The radius of a circle with circumference 62 centimeters.

Solution:

a.
$C = 2\pi \cdot r$	Write circumference formula.
$= 2 \cdot \pi \cdot 19$	Substitute 19 for r.
$= 38\pi$	Simplify.
≈ 119.39	Use a calculator.

The circumference is about 119.38 inches.

b.
$C = 2\pi \cdot r$	Write circumference formula.
$62 = 2 \cdot \pi \cdot r$	Substitute 62 for C.
$\dfrac{62}{2\pi} = r$	Divide each side by 2π.
$9.87 \approx r$	Use a calculator.

The radius is about 9.87 centimeters.

PRACTICE

Find the circumference of the circle with the given radius r.

1. $r = 5$ feet **2.** $r = 6.5$ yards **3.** $r = 18$ miles **4.** $r = 0.85$ mm

Find the radius of the circle with the given circumference C.

5. $C = 4$ miles **6.** $C = 9$ meters **7.** $C = \dfrac{\pi}{2}$ inches **8.** $C = 10$ units

BENCHMARK 5
(Chapters 10 and 11)

2. Find an Arc Length from an Angle Measure

Vocabulary   An **arc length** is a portion of the circumference of a circle.

EXAMPLE   **Find the length of each arc which does not contain the point *S*.**

The ratio of the length of an arc to the circumference of a circle is equal to the ratio of the arc's central angle to 360°.

a.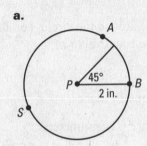

b.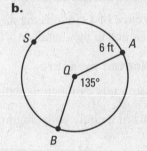

c.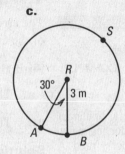

Solution:

a.   Arc length of $\overset{\frown}{AB} = \dfrac{45°}{360°} \cdot 2\pi(2) \approx 1.57$ inches.

b.   Arc length of $\overset{\frown}{AB} = \dfrac{135°}{360°} \cdot 2\pi(6) \approx 14.14$ feet.

c.   Arc length of $\overset{\frown}{AB} = \dfrac{30°}{360°} \cdot 2\pi(3) \approx 1.57$ m.

PRACTICE   **Find the length of an arc of a circle of radius *r* whose central angle is ∠*P*.**

9. $r = 5$ yds, $m\angle P = 35°$ **10.** $r = 7$ km, $m\angle P = 125°$

11. $r = 15$ ft, $m\angle P = 305°$ **12.** $r = 2$ light-years, $m\angle P = 90°$

3. Find the Area of a Circle

EXAMPLE   **Find the indicated measure.**

The area of a circle of radius *r* is proportional to the area of a square of side length *r*.

a. Area

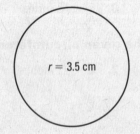

b. Diameter

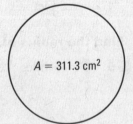

BENCHMARK 5
(Chapters 10 and 11)

Solution:

a. $A = \pi \cdot r^2$ Write formula for the area of a circle.

    $= \pi (3.5)^2$ Substitute 3.5 for r.

    $= 12.25\pi$ Simplify.

    ≈ 38.48 Use a calculator.

The area of the circle is about 38.48 centimeters.

b. $A = \pi \cdot r^2$ Write formula for the area of a circle.

    $311.3 = \pi \cdot r^2$ Substitute 311.3 for A.

    $\dfrac{311.3}{\pi} = r^2$ Divide both sides by π.

    $9.95 \approx r$ Find the positive square root of each side.

The radius of the circle is about 9.95 centimeters, so the diameter is about 19.9 centimeters.

PRACTICE   **Find the area of the circle with the given radius r.**

13. $r = 5$ feet   **14.** $r = 6.5$ yards   **15.** $r = 18$ miles   **16.** $r = 0.85$ mm

Find the radius of the circle with the given area A.

17. $A = 4$ miles^2 **18.** $A = 9$ meters^2 **19.** $A = \dfrac{\pi}{2}$ inches^2 **20.** $A = 10$ units^2

4. Find the Area of a Sector

Vocabulary   A **sector** of a circle is the region bounded by two radii of the circle and their intercepted arc.

EXAMPLE   **Find the area of the sectors formed by $\angle UTV$.**

Use the π key on your calculator and round at the end.

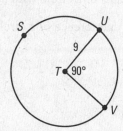

Step 1: Find the measures of the minor and major arcs.
Because $m\angle UTV = 90°$, $m\overset{\frown}{UV} = 90°$, and
$m\overset{\frown}{USV} = 360° - 90° = 270°$.

BENCHMARK 5
(Chapters 10 and 11)

Step 2: Find the areas of the small and large sectors.

$$\text{Area of small sector} = \frac{m\widehat{UV}}{360°} \cdot \pi \cdot r^2 \qquad \text{Write formula for area of a sector.}$$

$$= \frac{90°}{360°} \cdot \pi \cdot 9^2 \qquad \text{Substitute.}$$

$$\approx 63.62 \qquad \text{Use a calculator.}$$

$$\text{Area of large sector} = \frac{m\widehat{USV}}{360°} \cdot \pi \cdot r^2 \qquad \text{Write formula for area of a sector.}$$

$$= \frac{270°}{360°} \cdot \pi \cdot 9^2 \qquad \text{Substitute.}$$

$$\approx 190.85 \qquad \text{Use a calculator.}$$

The areas of the small and large sectors are about 63.62 square units and 190.85 square units, respectively.

PRACTICE   **Find the area of the sector of a circle with the given radius and intercepted arc measure.**

21. $r = 8, 80°$ **22.** $r = 6, 36°$ **23.** $r = 16, 60°$

24. $r = 4, 45°$ **25.** $r = 10, 30°$ **26.** $r = 7, 180°$

Quiz

Round all answers to the nearest hundredth.

1. Find the circumference of a circle with radius 10 inches.

2. Find the radius of a circle with circumference 12 inches.

3. Find the arc length and area of a sector of a circle with radius 6 meters whose central angle is 30°.

4. Find the area of a circle with radius 12 cm.

5. Find the radius of a circle with area 12 cm².

6. Find the circumference of a circle with area 12 cm².

BENCHMARK 5
(Chapters 10 and 11)

D. Solids

Many objects in the physical world can be idealized as polyhedrons, so we study such solids and their properties.

1. Identify and Name Solids

Vocabulary   A **polyhedron** is a solid that is bounded by polygons, called **faces**, that enclose a single region of space. An **edge** of a polyhedron is a line segment formed by the intersection of two faces. A **vertex** of a polyhedron is a point where three or more edges meet.

EXAMPLE

A polyhedron may be neither a prism nor a pyramid.

Tell whether the solid is a polyhedron. If it is, name the polyhedron and find the number of faces, vertices, and edges.

a.

b.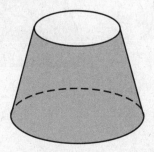

c.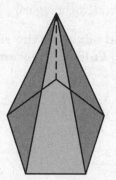

Solution:

a.   The solid is formed by polygons, so it is a polyhedron. The two bases are congruent hexagons, so it is a hexagonal prism. It has 8 faces, 12 vertices, and 18 edges.

b.   The solid is formed by slicing the tip off a cone, so it is not a polyhedron.

c.   The solid is formed by polygons, so it is a polyhedron. The base is a pentagon, so it is a pentagonal pyramid. It has 6 faces, consisting of 1 base, 3 visible triangular faces, and 2 non-visible triangular faces. The polyhedron has 6 faces, 6 vertices, and 10 edges.

BENCHMARK 5
(Chapters 10 and 11)

PRACTICE   Tell whether the solid is a polyhedron. If it is, name the polyhedron and find the number of faces, vertices, and edges.

1.
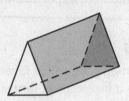

2.
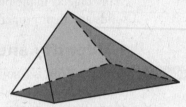

3.
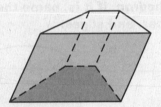

4.
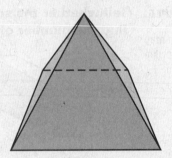

2. Use Euler's Theorem

Vocabulary   A polyhedron is **regular** if all of its faces are congruent regular polygons.

EXAMPLE   **Find the number of faces, vertices, and edges of the regular tetrahedron. Check your answer using Euler's Theorem.**

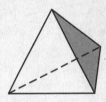

Solution:

Use Euler's formula to check if your sketch of a solid is accurate.

By counting on the diagram, the tetrahedron has 4 faces, 4 vertices, and 6 edges. Use Euler's Theorem to check.

$F + V = E + 2$	**Euler's Theorem.**
$4 + 4 = 6 + 2$	**Substitute.**
$8 = 8$	**This is a true statement. So the solution checks.**

Copyright © by McDougal Littell, a division of Houghton Mifflin Company.

BENCHMARK 5
(Chapters 10 and 11)

PRACTICE   You found the number of faces, vertices, and edges of the polyhedra in the previous section. Now check your answers using Euler's theorem.

5.
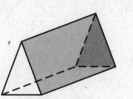

6.
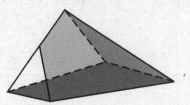

7.
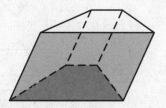

8.
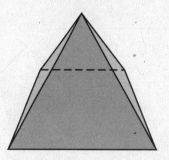

3. Describe Cross Sections

Vocabulary   The intersection of a plane and a solid is called a **cross section**.

EXAMPLE   **Describe the shaped formed by the intersection of the plane *P* and the right prism whose bases are equilateral triangles.**

Shading different faces in varying shades of gray helps to make your sketches more understandable.

a.
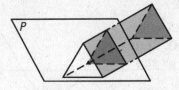

b.
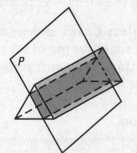

c.
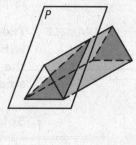

Solution:

a. The cross section is an equilateral triangle.

b. The cross section is a rectangle.

c. The cross section is an isosceles triangle.

BENCHMARK 5
(Chapters 10 and 11)

PRACTICE   Describe the intersection of the plane and the solid.

9.

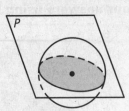

10.

11.

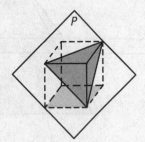

12.

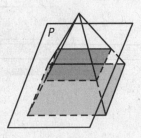

4. Use the Scale Factor of Similar Solids

Vocabulary   Two solids of the same type with equal ratios of corresponding linear measures, such as heights or radii, are called **similar** solids. The common ratio is called the **scale** factor of one solid to the other solid.

EXAMPLE   **The lidless boxes shown are similar with a scale factor of 63 : 100. Find the surface area and volume of the smaller box.**

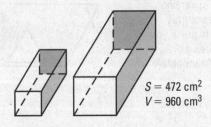

$S = 472 \text{ cm}^2$
$V = 960 \text{ cm}^3$

Solution:

Area varies as the square of the length, volume varies as the cube of the length.

Let S_1 and V_1 denote the surface area and volume, respectively, of the smaller box.

Use Theorem 12.13 to write two proportions:

$$\frac{S_1}{S} = \frac{a^2}{b^2} \qquad\qquad \frac{V_1}{V} = \frac{a^3}{b^3}$$

$$\frac{S_1}{472} = \frac{63^2}{100^2} \qquad\qquad \frac{V_1}{960} = \frac{63^3}{100^3}$$

Solving, we obtain $S_1 \approx 187.34$ and $V_1 \approx 240.05$. So, the surface area of the smaller box is about 187.34 square centimeters, and the volume of the smaller box is about 240.05 cubic centimeters.

BENCHMARK 5
(Chapters 10 and 11)

PRACTICE   **You are given the scale factor for a pair of similar solids and the surface area *S* and volume *V* of the smaller solid. Find the surface area S_1 and volume V_1 of the larger solid in each case.**

13. $3 : 4$, $S = 102$ cm^2, $V = 326$ cm^3 **14.** $13 : 40$, $S = 210$ m^2, $V = 697$ m^3

15. $1 : 4$, $S = 56$ in.^{2}, $V = 89$ in.^{3} **16.** $12 : 45$, $S = 2.56$ miles^2, $V = 7.08$ miles^3

Quiz

1. Find the values of F, E, and V in Euler's Formula for a hexagonal prism.

2. Find the values of F, E, and V in Euler's Formula for a decagonal pyramid.

3. Describe the possible cross-sections of a cube.

4. A plane intersects a pentagonal prism parallel to its base in such a way that the ratio of volumes is $8 : 27$.

a. What is the scale factor?

b. If the surface area of the smaller prism is 400, then what is the surface area of the larger prism?

BENCHMARK 5
(Chapters 10 and 11)

E. Spheres, Pyramids, and Cones

1. Find the Surface Area of a Sphere

Vocabulary A **sphere** is the set of all points in space equidistant from a given point, called the **center** of the sphere.

EXAMPLE **Find the surface area of the sphere.**

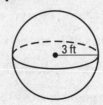

Solution:

A circle is to two dimensions as a sphere is to three dimensions.

$S = 4\pi \cdot r^2$ Formula for surface area of a sphere.

$= 4\pi(3)^2$ Substitute 3 for r.

$= 36\pi$ Simplify.

≈ 113.10 Use a calculator.

The surface area of the sphere is approximately 113.10 square feet.

PRACTICE **Either the surface area S or the radius r of a sphere is given. Find the other value. Round your answers to the nearest hundredth.**

1. $S = 256$ cm^2 2. $S = 3049$ m^2 3. $r = 19$ inches

4. $r = \pi$ yards   5. $r = \frac{3}{8}$ miles   6. $S = \pi$ feet^2

2. Find the Volume of a Pyramid and Cone

EXAMPLE **Find the volume of the solid.**

The volume formulas given in Theorems 12.9 and 12.10 apply to both right and oblique pyramids and cones.

a.
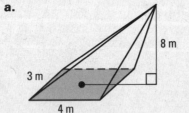

b.
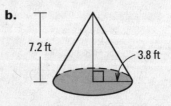

Solution:

a. $V = \frac{1}{3}B \cdot h$

$= \frac{1}{3}(3 \cdot 4)(8)$

$= 32$ m^3

b. $V = \frac{1}{3}B \cdot h$

$= \frac{1}{3}(\pi \cdot r^2)h$

$= \frac{1}{3}(\pi \cdot 3.8^2)(7.2)$

$= 34.656\pi$

≈ 108.88 ft^3

BENCHMARK 5
(Chapters 10 and 11)

PRACTICE   **Find the volume of each pyramid or cone.**

7.

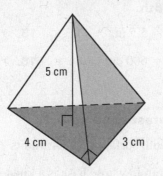

5 cm

4 cm   3 cm

8.

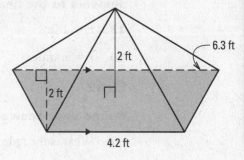

2 ft

6.3 ft

2 ft

4.2 ft

9.

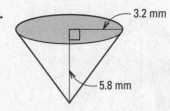

3.2 mm

5.8 mm

10.

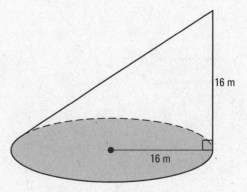

16 m

16 m

11.

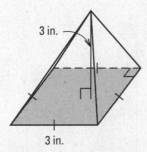

3 in.

3 in.

12.

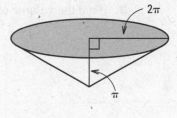

2π

π

3. Find the Volume of a Sphere

EXAMPLE   **A spherical scoop of ice cream has a diameter of 2.5 inches. What is the volume of two scoops?**

Solution:

A hemisphere results from cutting a sphere precisely in half.

The diameter of the scoop is 2.5 inches, so the radius is $\frac{2.5}{2} = 1.25$ inches. Find the volume of each scoop:

$V = \frac{4}{3} \pi \cdot r^3$ **Formula for volume of a sphere.**

$= \frac{4}{3} \pi (1.25)^3$ **Substitute.**

≈ 8.18 **Use a calculator to simplify.**

There are two scoops, so the total volume of ice cream is about $2 \cdot 8.18 = 16.36$ cubic inches.

BENCHMARK 5

(Chapters 10 and 11)

PRACTICE **Find the volume of the sphere with the given radius. Round your answers to the nearest hundredth.**

13. $r = 2$ ft   **14.** $r = 5.5$ in.   **15.** $r = 6.3$ mm

16. $r = \pi$ miles   **17.** $r = 600$ cm   **18.** $r = 72$ m

Quiz

Round your answers to the nearest hundredth.

1. What is the radius of a sphere with surface area 24π units²?

2. Find the volume of the right pyramid whose base is a kite.

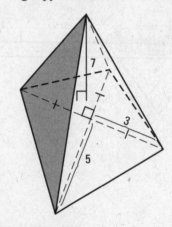

3. Find the volume of the right cone.

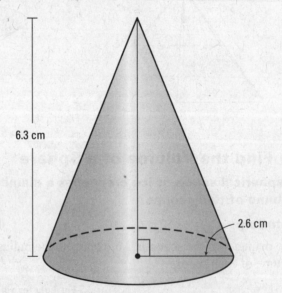

4. Find the radius of a sphere whose volume is 264π m³.

BENCHMARK 6
(Chapter 12)

A. Probabilities of Simple and Compound Events

The **probability of an event** is a measure of the likelihood that the event will occur. The following examples describe how to find a **theoretical probability** and **odds** of an event occurring, and how to find the probabilities of **compound** events that are **independent** and **dependent**.

1. Find a Theoretical Probability

Vocabulary

Outcome A possible result of an experiment.

Event An outcome or a collection of outcomes.

Sample space The set of all possible outcomes.

Favorable outcomes The outcomes for a specified event.

Theoretical probability When all outcomes are equally likely, the theoretical probability $P(A)$ of event A is found by: $P(A) = \dfrac{\text{Number of favorable outcomes}}{\text{Total number of outcomes}}$.

EXAMPLE

A bag contains 5 red, 6 blue, 4 green, and 9 yellow marbles. A student reaches in the bag and chooses a marble at random. What is the probability that the student chooses a yellow marble?

When an object is chosen *at random*, all choices are equally likely.

Solution:

The bag holds a total of $5 + 6 + 4 + 9 = 24$ marbles. So, there are 24 possible outcomes. Of all the marbles, 9 are yellow. There are 9 favorable outcomes.

$$P(\text{yellow marble}) = \frac{\text{Number of favorable outcomes}}{\text{Total number of outcomes}}$$

$$= \frac{\text{Number of yellow marbles}}{\text{Total number of marbles}} = \frac{9}{24} = \frac{3}{8}$$

PRACTICE

A soccer coach has a box that contains 3 small, 6 medium, 7 large, and 4 extra-large soccer jerseys. A player chooses a jersey at random. Find the probability that the player chooses a jersey of the given size.

  1. small   **2.** medium   **3.** large   **4.** extra-large

2. Find the Odds

Vocabulary

Odds are read as the ratio of one number to another. The odds here are read as "five to one." Odds are usually written as $a : b$.

Odds The odds of an event compare the number of favorable and unfavorable outcomes when all outcomes are equally likely.

Odds in favor $= \dfrac{\text{Number of favorable outcomes}}{\text{Number of unfavorable outcomes}}$

Odds against $= \dfrac{\text{Number of unfavorable outcomes}}{\text{Number of favorable outcomes}}$

BENCHMARK 6
(Chapter 12)

EXAMPLE **A number cube is rolled. Find the odds against a 4 being rolled.**

Solution:

The 6 possible outcomes are all equally likely. The one favorable outcome is a roll of 4. Rolling the other numbers are unfavorable outcomes.

$$\text{Odds against rolling a } 4 = \frac{\text{Number of unfavorable outcomes}}{\text{Number of favorable outcomes}} = \frac{5}{1} \text{ or } 5 : 1$$

PRACTICE **A standard deck of 52 cards is shuffled and a card is drawn at random. Find the odds in favor of and against each of the following events.**

5. a red ace is drawn

6. a 6 is drawn

7. a spade is drawn

8. a face card is drawn

3. Use the Permutation Formula

Vocabulary *n* **factorial** For any positive integer n, the product of the integers from 1 to n, written as $n!$

Permutation An arrangement of objects in which order is important;

number of permutations of n objects: $_nP_n = n!$

number of permutations of n objects taken r at a time, where $r \leq n$:

$$_nP_r = \frac{n!}{(n-r)!}$$

EXAMPLE **You borrow 10 books from the school library for a research project. You can only fit 4 in your backpack, so you leave the rest in the classroom. In how many ways can you arrange the remaining books on a classroom bookshelf?**

Solution:

To find the number of permutations of 6 books chosen from 10, find $_{10}P_6$.

$_{10}P_6 = \dfrac{10!}{(10-6)!}$ **Permutations formula**

Expand the factorial only as far as necessary. In this case, 4! is a factor of 10!.

$= \dfrac{10!}{4!}$ **Subtract.**

$= \dfrac{10 \cdot 9 \cdot 8 \cdot 7 \cdot 6 \cdot 5 \cdot \cancel{4!}}{\cancel{4!}}$ **Expand factorials.**
    Divide out common factor, 4!.

$= 151,200$ **Multiply.**

There are 151,200 ways to arrange 6 books out of 10.

PRACTICE **Find the number of ways you can arrange the number of letters in the word.**

9. DOG, 2 of the letters

10. ORANGE, 4 of the letters

11. JULY, 3 of the letters

12. PICTURE, 6 of the letters

BENCHMARK 6
(Chapter 12)

4. Use the Combination Formula

Vocabulary

Combination A selection of objects in which order is not important; number of combinations of n objects taken r at a time, where $r \leq n$:

$$_nC_r = \frac{n!}{(n-r)! \cdot r!}$$

You order a sundae at a yogurt shop. You can choose 3 toppings from a list of 9. How many combinations of toppings are possible?

Solution:

The order in which you choose the toppings is not important. So, to find the number of combinations of 9 toppings taken 3 at a time, find $_9C_3$.

$$_9C_3 = \frac{9!}{(9-3)! \cdot 3!}$$ **Permutations formula**

$$= \frac{9!}{6! \cdot 3!}$$ **Subtract.**

$$= \frac{9 \cdot 8 \cdot 7 \cdot \cancel{6!}}{\cancel{6!} \cdot (3 \cdot 2 \cdot 1)}$$ **Expand factorials.**
Divide out common factor, 6!.

$$= 84$$ **Simplify.**

There are 84 different combinations of toppings you can choose.

PRACTICE

A pizza shop offers a daily special where customers can choose a number of toppings from a list of toppings available that day. Find the number of possible combinations for each daily special.

13. choose 2 toppings from 6 toppings   **14.** choose 3 toppings from 8 toppings

15. choose 1 topping from 5 toppings   **16.** choose 4 toppings from 10 toppings

5. Find the Probability of a Compound Event

Vocabulary

Compound event A combination of two or more events, using the word *and* or the word *or*.

Mutually exclusive events Events that have no common outcomes:

$$P(A \text{ or } B) = P(A) + P(B).$$

Overlapping events Events that have at least one common outcome:

$$P(A \text{ or } B) = P(A) + P(B) - P(A \text{ and } B).$$

EXAMPLE

Draw a Venn diagram to help you understand mutual and overlapping events.

You roll a number cube. Find the probability that you roll a number greater than 4 or an odd number.

Solution:

Because 5 is both a number greater than 4 and an odd number, rolling a number greater than 4 and an odd number are overlapping events. There are 2 numbers greater than 4, 3 odd numbers, and 1 number that is both.

$$P(\text{greater than 4 or odd}) = P(\text{greater than 4}) + P(\text{odd}) - P(\text{greater than 4 and odd})$$

$$= \frac{2}{6} + \frac{3}{6} - \frac{1}{6} = \frac{4}{6} = \frac{2}{3}$$

BENCHMARK 6
(Chapter 12)

PRACTICE **You roll a number cube. Find the probability of each outcome.**

17. a number less than 4 or an odd number

18. a multiple of 3 or a prime number

19. an odd number or a number greater than 3

6. Find the Probability of Independent and Dependent Events

Vocabulary **Independent events** Two events are independent events if the occurrence of one event has no effect on the occurrence of the other. $P(A \text{ and } B) = P(A) \cdot P(B)$.

Dependent events Two events are dependent events if the occurrence of one event affects the occurrence of the other. $P(A \text{ and } B) = P(A) \cdot P(B \text{ given } A)$.

EXAMPLE **A box contains 6 red markers and 3 green markers. You choose one marker at random, do not replace it, then choose a second marker at random. What is the probability that both markers are red?**

After one item is chosen and not replaced, reduce the total number remaining by 1.

Solution:

Because you do not replace the first marker, the events are dependent. Before you choose a marker, there are 9 markers, and 6 of them are red. After you choose a red marker, there are 8 markers left, and 5 of them are red.

$P(\text{red and then red}) = P(\text{red}) \cdot P(\text{red given red})$

$$= \frac{6}{9} \cdot \frac{5}{8} = \frac{30}{72} = \frac{5}{12}$$

PRACTICE **A bag contains 5 blue, 4 red, and 3 green marbles. You randomly draw 2 marbles, one at a time. Find the probability:**

20. of drawing a red marble, which you replace, and then drawing a green marble

21. of drawing two blue marbles without replacement

22. of drawing a green marble, which you do not replace, and then drawing a blue marble

Quiz

A jar on a store counter contains pens of 5 different colors. The jar contains 6 red pens, 8 blue pens, 4 green pens, 10 black pens, and 2 purple pens. A customer reaches into the jar and chooses a pen at random. Find the probability that the customer chooses a pen of the given color.

1. red   **2.** green   **3.** black   **4.** purple

A standard deck of 52 cards is shuffled and a card is drawn at random. Find the odds in favor of and against each of the following events.

5. a 9 is drawn   **6.** a 3 of diamonds is drawn

7. a black king is drawn   **8.** a red card is drawn

BENCHMARK 6
(Chapter 12)

Find the number of ways you can arrange the given number of letters in the word.

9. THIS, 2 of the letters

10. BLACK, 3 of the letters

11. BIKE, 4 of the letters

12. MOTHERS, 5 of the letters

Students are being selected for various school awards. Find the number of possible combinations for each award given the number of each award and the number of students nominated.

13. 2 students from 5 nominated

14. 4 students from 6 nominated

15. 2 students from 11 nominated

16. 3 students from 7 nominated

You roll a number cube. Find the probability of each outcome.

17. a number less than 5 or an even number

18. an odd number or a prime number

A bag contains 7 blue, 4 red, and 5 green marbles. You randomly draw 2 marbles, one at a time. Find the probability:

19. of drawing a red marble, which you replace, and then drawing a blue marble

20. of drawing two green marbles without replacement

21. of drawing a red marble, which you do not replace, and then drawing a green marble

Answers

Benchmark 1

A. Line Segments

1–11. Answers will vary. Samples are given.

1. *BAC* **2.** $\overleftrightarrow{DE}$, $\overleftrightarrow{FE}$, $\overleftrightarrow{ED}$ **3.** *A, G, C* **4.** Yes

5. No **6.** $\overrightarrow{ED}$ and $\overrightarrow{EF}$, $\overrightarrow{GA}$ and $\overrightarrow{GC}$

7.

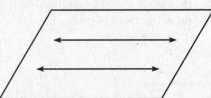

8.
9.

10.

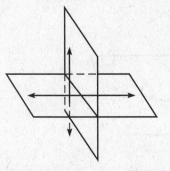

11.

12. Yes; think of the corner of a room where two walls and the ceiling meet. **13.** $\overline{AO}$ or $\overline{OC}$

14. No **15.** $\overline{AC}$ **16.** $\overline{OB}$

17. $\overline{AO} \cong \overline{OC}$ and $\overline{EO} \cong \overline{EB}$ **18.** Yes

19. $\left(\frac{5}{2}, \frac{5}{2}\right)$ **20.** $\left(\frac{3}{2}, -\frac{3}{2}\right)$ **21.** (2.35, 0.95)

22. $\left(-\frac{1}{5}, \frac{5}{3}\right)$ **23.** (3, 2) **24.** (−4, −8) **25.** 1.4

26. 7.6 **27.** 14.3 **28.** 1.7 **29.** 8 **30.** 2|*a*|

Quiz

1. *ABD* **2.** *B* **3.** *C, D,* or *E* **4.** $\overline{BC}$ **5.** (5, 1)

6. $2\sqrt{10}$ **7.** $2\sqrt{10}$ **8.** Yes

B. Angles

1–3. Answers may vary. Samples are given.

1. ∠*HBD*, ∠*CBH* **2.** ∠*HAB*, ∠*FAE* **3.** 80°, 135° **4.** No **5.** 7 **6.** 7 **7.** Yes **8.** 20

9. No **10.** No **11.** 0 **12.** No

13–15. Answers may vary. Samples are given.

13. ∠*BFE*, ∠*CDE* **14.** ∠*DEC*, ∠*ABF*

15. ∠*DEF* **16.** 50° **17.** They are congruent.

18. 15 **19.** $m\angle F = 60°$, $m\angle H = 150°$

20. $m\angle F = 48°$, $m\angle H = 60°$

21. $m\angle F = 71.5°$, $m\angle H = 54.8°$

22. $m\angle F = 45°$, $m\angle H = 90°$ **23.** $m\angle F = 30°$, $m\angle H = 135°$ **24.** $m\angle F = 1°$, $m\angle H = 120°$

25. ∠4 and ∠2 **26.** ∠4 and ∠2 **27.** ∠6 and ∠8

28. ∠9 and ∠11

Quiz

1. ∠*ABF*, ∠*EBC* **2.** ∠*CBD*, ∠*DBA* **3.** ∠*CBF*

4. 20 **5.** 140° **6.** ∠*ABD*, ∠*FBC*

7. ∠*FBD*, $\overrightarrow{BC}$ **8.** ∠*ABE* ≅ ∠*FBC*

C. Polygons

1.

2.

3.

4.

5.

6.

7.

8.

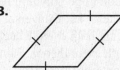

9.

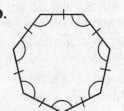

10.

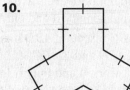

11.

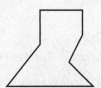

12.

13. $C = 94.2$ cm, $A = 706.5$ cm²

14. $C = 75.4$ mi, $A = 452.2$ mi^2 **15.** $C = 785$ m, $A = 49,062.5$ m^2
16. $C = 136.9$ in., $A = 1492.3$ in.^{2}
17. $C = 18.8$ yd, $A = 28.3$ yd^2
18. $C = 188.4$ ft, $A = 2826$ ft^2

Quiz

1. a concave nonagon   **2.** convex, equilangular, equilateral, regular hexagon   **3.** a convex, equiangular, equilateral, regular triangle   **4.** a concave, equilateral octagon   **5.** $C = 50.2$ ft, $A = 201.0$ ft^2 **6.** $C = 91.1$ cm, $A = 660.2$ cm^2

D. Inductive and Deductive Reasoning

1. o   **2.** ↑   **3.** ⊗ ⊗ ⊗ ⊗   **4.** ⎾   **5.** 36   **6.** 13
7. deabc   **8.** Monday   **9.** The product of any number with zero is zero.   **10.** There are 720 different arrangements.   **11.** They determine at most ten lines.   **12.** A number is divisible by three only if the sum of its digits is divisible by three.   **13.** A car in the school parking lot which is not red.   **14.** $x = \frac{1}{2}$ **15.** Viktor has red hair but either does not have green eyes or does not have freckles.   **16.** 5 and $\frac{1}{5}$ **17.** Converse: If a number is an integer, then it is even. False. Inverse: If a number is not even, then it is not an integer. False. Contrapositive: If a number is not an integer, then it is not even. True.
18. Converse: If I open my umbrella, then it will rain. False. Inverse: If it doesn't rain, then I will not open my umbrella. True. Contrapositive: If I don't open my umbrella, then it is not raining. True.   **19.** Converse: If $n + m$ is even, then n and m are both even. False. Inverse: If n and m are not both even, then $n + m$ is not even. False. Contrapositive: If $n + m$ is not even, then n and m are not both even. True.   **20.** $\angle A$ and $\angle B$ are complementary if and only if $m\angle A + m\angle B = 90°$.
21. $\overrightarrow{BC}$ bisects $\angle ABD$ if and only if $\overrightarrow{BC}$ is interior to $\angle ABD$ and $\angle ABC \cong \angle CBD$.
22. I work if and only if I am paid.   **23.** $BA + AC = BC$ **24.** A, B, and C determine a plane.
25. If I am sad, my nose runs.   **26.** If I do my homework, we will have fun.

Quiz

1. $\frac{1}{81}$ **2.** There are 6 handshakes.   **3.** $x = -2$
4. If-Then: If it is a dog, then it barks. Converse: If it barks, then it is a dog. Inverse: If it is not a

dog, then it does not bark. Contrapositive: If it does not bark, then it is not a dog.
5. M is the midpoint of the line segment with endpoints (x_1, y_1) and (x_2, y_2) if and only if the coordinates of M are $\left(\dfrac{x_1 + x_2}{2}, \dfrac{y_1 + y_2}{2} \right)$.
6. $\angle A$ is acute.   **7.** No; neither of the statements has a conclusion which is the hypothesis of the other.

E. Writing Proofs

1. Postulate 5: Through any two points there is exactly one line.   **2.** Postulate 10: If two points lie in a plane, then the line containing them lies in the plane.   **3.** Planes P and Q intersect in line ℓ.
4. Lines ℓ and m intersect in point A.

5.

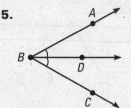

6.

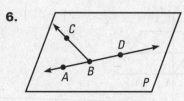

7.

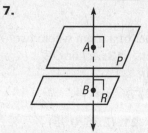

8.

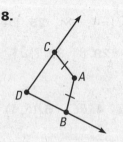

Answers continued

9.

Equation	Explanation	Reason
$2x + 3 = 7$	Write original equation.	Given
$2x = 4$	Subtract 3 from each side.	Subtraction Property
$x = 2$	Divide each side by 2.	Division Property

10.

Equation	Explanation	Reason
$-2 + x = 12 - 3x$	Write original equation.	Given
$-2 + 4x = 12$	Add $3x$ to each side.	Addition Property
$4x = 14$	Add 2 to each side.	Addition Property
$x = \dfrac{14}{4}$	Divide each side by 4.	Division Property
$x = \dfrac{7}{2}$	Replace $\dfrac{14}{4}$ by $\dfrac{7}{2}$.	Substitution Property

11.

Equation	Explanation	Reason
$3(x + 1) = 9$	Write original equation.	Given
$3x + 3 = 9$	Multiply.	Distributive Property
$3x = 6$	Subtract 3 from each side.	Subtraction Property
$x = 2$	Divide each side by 3.	Division Property

12.

Equation	Explanation	Reason
$4(2x + 6) = -3(8 + x)$	Write original equation.	Given
$8x + 24 = -24 - 3x$	Multiply.	Distributive Property
$11x + 24 = -24$	Add $3x$ to each side.	Addition Property
$11x = -48$	Subtract 24 from each side.	Subtraction Property
$x = -\dfrac{48}{11}$	Divide each side by 11.	Division Property

13. Segment Addition Postulate; Substitution Property of Equality; Subtraction Property of Equality; Division Property of Equality

14. Given: M is the midpoint of $\overline{AB}$ and N is the midpoint of $\overline{AM}$

Prove: a. $4NM = AB$ and

b. $NM = \dfrac{1}{4}AB$

Statements	Reasons
1. M is the midpoint of $\overline{AB}$ and N is the midpoint of $\overline{AM}$	**1.** Given
2. $\overline{AM} \cong \overline{MB}$; $\overline{AN} \cong \overline{NM}$	**2.** Definition of midpoint
3. $AM = MB$; $AN = NM$	**3.** Definition of congruent segments
4. $AM + MB = AB$; $AN + NM = AM$	**4.** Segment Addition Postulate
5. $AM + AM = AB$; $NM + NM = AM$	**5.** Substitution Property of Equality
6. $NM + NM + NM + NM = AB$	**6.** Substitution Property of Equality
7. $4NM = AB$	**7.** Distributive Property
8. $NM = \dfrac{1}{4}AB$	**8.** Division Property of Equality

Geometry
Benchmark Answer Key **A3**

Answers continued

15. The distance between Alma and Nelson is the same as the distance between Nelson and Winona.

16. $m\angle 2 = 129°$, $m\angle 3 = 51°$, $m\angle 4 = 129°$

17. $m\angle 1 = m\angle 3 = 31°$, $m\angle 4 = 149°$

18. $m\angle 1 = 15°$, $m\angle 2 = m\angle 4 = 165°$

19. $m\angle 1 = 45°$, $m\angle 2 = 135°$, $m\angle 3 = 45°$

Quiz

1.

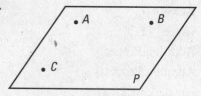

2.

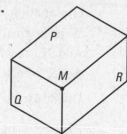

3.

Equation	Explanation	Reason
$9x + 3 = 21$	Write original equation.	Given
$9x = 18$	Subtract 3 from each side.	Subtraction Property
$x = 2$	Divide each side by 9.	Division Property

4. Given: $\overrightarrow{AB}$ bisects $\angle CAD$ and $\overrightarrow{AE}$ bisects $\angle BAD$
   Prove: $m\angle CAD = 4m\angle EAD$

Statements	Reasons
1. $\overrightarrow{AB}$ bisects $\angle CAD$ and $\overrightarrow{AE}$ bisects $\angle BAD$	**1.** Given
2. $\angle CAB \cong \angle BAD$; $\angle BAE \cong \angle EAD$	**2.** Definition of angle bisector
3. $m\angle CAB = m\angle BAD$; $m\angle BAE = m\angle EAD$	**3.** Definition of congruent angles
4. $m\angle CAB + m\angle BAD = m\angle CAD$; $m\angle BAE + m\angle EAD = m\angle BAD$	**4.** Angle Addition Postulate
5. $m\angle BAD + m\angle BAD = m\angle CAD$; $m\angle EAD + m\angle EAD = m\angle BAD$	**5.** Substitution Property of Equality
6. $m\angle EAD + m\angle EAD + m\angle EAD + m\angle EAD = m\angle CAD$	**6.** Substitution Property of Equality
7. $4m\angle EAD = m\angle CAD$	**7.** Distributive Property

5. $m\angle 1 = m\angle 2 = m\angle 4 = 15°$; $m\angle 3 = m\angle 5 = 75°$

Answer Key

Benchmark 2

A. Parallel and Perpendicular Lines

1. $\overleftrightarrow{CD}, \overleftrightarrow{AB}, \overleftrightarrow{EF}$　**2.** $\overleftrightarrow{CG}$　**3.** $\overleftrightarrow{GH}$ and $\overleftrightarrow{HD}$

4. BEF　**5.** Alternate exterior　**6.** Alternate interior　**7.** Corresponding　**8.** Consecutive interior　**9.** $m\angle 3 = 40°$ by the Vertical Angles Congruence Theorem; $m\angle 5 = 40°$ by the Corresponding Angles Postulate; $m\angle 7 = 40°$ by the Corresponding Angles Postulate.
10. $x = 10$　**11.** Yes, by Consecutive Interior Angles Converse　**12.** Yes, by Alternate Interior Angles Converse　**13.** It is not possible to prove that $p \parallel q$ with the information given.
14. No　**15.** No　**16.** No　**17.** $\ell \parallel m, p \parallel q$
18. p is perpendicular to n and ℓ is perpendicular to r.　**19.** $2\sqrt{2}$　**20.** $2\sqrt{2}$　**21.** $(1, 2)$; 2.2
22. $(3, 1)$; 3.2

Quiz

1.

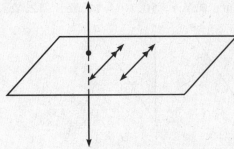

2.

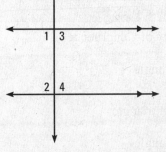

3. $m\angle 2 = 143°$ by the Consecutive Interior Angles Theorem; $m\angle 3 = 143°$ by the definition of supplementary angles; $m\angle 4 = 37°$ by the Alternate Interior Angles Theorem　**4.** No. The sum of the measures of the consecutive interior angles is not 180°, so $p \nparallel q$ by the contrapositive of the Consecutive Interior Angles theorem.　**5.** 0.39

B. Equations of Lines

1. -3　**2.** 0　**3.** -1　**4.** $-\dfrac{1}{3}$　**5.** 0
6. undefined　**7.** perpendicular　**8.** neither
9. perpendicular

10.

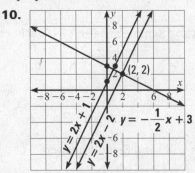

11. $y = -x + 3$　**12a.** $y = 2x$　**12b.** $y = \dfrac{1}{3}x$

13.

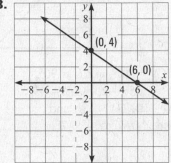

14.

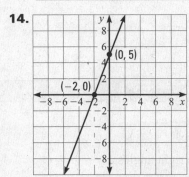

15.

Answers continued

Quiz

1. $y = x$ **2.** $y = -x + 4$ **3.** Yes
4. $y = x - 3$ **5.** $y = -x + 1$
6. (4, 0) and (0, −2) **7.** No

C. Triangles

1. Answers will vary. Sample answer:

2. Not possible
3 and 4. Answers will vary. Sample answer:

3.  **4.**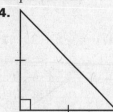

5. $m\angle M = 44°, m\angle N = 46°, m\angle L = 90°$
6. $m\angle R = 5°, m\angle P = 35°$ **7.** $m\angle S = 49°,$
$m\angle T = 49°$ **8.** 70° **9.** $\overline{DN} \cong \overline{SN}$ and
$\angle NCD \cong \angle NRS$ and $\angle DNC \cong \angle SNR$

10. $\overline{SN}$ **11.** 50° **12.** $x = 45, y = 22.5$
13. $x = 12, y = 5$ **14.** $x = 9, y = 35$
15. $x = 6, y = 35$

Quiz

1. 11 **2.** 76° **3.** No; an acute triangle has
3 acute angles. **4.** 20° **5.** 8

D. Proving Triangles are Congruent

1. $x = 2, y = 27, z = 45°$ **2.** *PWURS* **3.** It is
given that $\overline{AB} \cong \overline{EB}$, $\overline{AC} \cong \overline{ED}$, and $\overline{CB} \cong \overline{DB}$.
Since $\overleftrightarrow{AC} \parallel \overleftrightarrow{ED}$, we have that $\angle A \cong \angle E$ and
$\angle C \cong \angle D$ since these are all alternate interior
angles formed by the transversals $\overleftrightarrow{AE}$ and $\overleftrightarrow{DC}$,
respectively. Now $\angle CBA \cong \angle DBE$ since vertical
angles are congruent. **4.** $\overrightarrow{HG}$ bisects $\angle IHJ$
5. False; $\triangle DFG \cong \triangle JHK$
6. True; SSS Congruence Postulate
7. True; SSS Congruence Postulate **8.** False;
we don't know that corresponding sides are
congruent **9.** Yes **10.** No **11.** Yes **12.** Yes
13.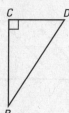

14.

Statements	Reasons
H 1. $\overline{DB} \cong \overline{DB}$	**1.** Reflexive Property of Congruence
2. $\angle BAD$ and $\angle DCB$ are right angles	**2.** Definition of rectangle
3. $\triangle ABD$ and $\triangle CDB$ are right triangles	**3.** Definition of right triangle
L 4. $\overline{AD} \cong \overline{CB}$	**4.** Definition of rectangle
5. $\triangle ABD \cong \triangle CDB$	**5.** HL Congruence Theorem

15.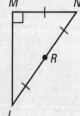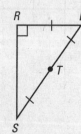

16.

Statements	Reasons
L 1. $\overline{MN} \cong \overline{RL}$	1. Given
2. $\overline{MN} \perp \overline{ML}$; $\overline{SR} \perp \overline{RL}$	2. Given
3. $\angle NML$ and $\angle LRS$ are right angles.	3. Definition of $\perp$ lines
4. $\triangle MNL$ and $\triangle RLS$ are right triangles.	4. Definition of right triangle
5. $NR = RL = LT = TS$	5. Given
6. $NR + RL = NL$; $LT + TS = LS$	6. Segment Addition Postulate
7. $NL = LS$	7. Substitution Property of Equality
H 8. $\overline{NL} \cong \overline{LS}$	8. Definition of congruent segments
9. $\triangle MNL = \triangle RLS$	9. HL Congruence Theorem

17. $\triangle ABC \cong \triangle CDA$; ASA Postulate
18. $x = \dfrac{20}{3}$ **19.** $x = 2$ **20.** No
21a. $\overline{PQ} \parallel \overline{RS}$ **21b.** Given   **21c.** $\angle RPQ$
21d. $\angle PRQ$ **21e.** Alternate Interior Angles
Congruence Theorem   **21f.** $\overline{RP}$ **21g.** AAS
Congruence Theorem   **22.** $\triangle CDB \cong \triangle EBD$,
by AAS   **23.** $\triangle EAD \cong \triangle CBD$, by AAS
24. $\triangle LOP \cong \triangle NOP$, by SAS
25. $\triangle XYZ \cong \triangle YXW$, by HL Theorem

Quiz

1. $\triangle XYW \cong \triangle ZWY$, SSS   **2.** $\triangle AGC \cong \triangle FBH$,
SSS   **3.** $\triangle PRS \cong \triangle TVS$, SAS
4. $\triangle GHI \cong \triangle GHJ$, AAS   **5.** No. One triangle
could have all sides of length 1 inch and the other
of 1 foot.   **6.** No. Two right triangles with hypot-
enuses of the same length could have different
leg lengths.

E: Congruence Transformations

1. translation; congruent   **2.** reflection or
rotation and translation; congruent   **3.** none;
although the corresponding angles are congruent, the corresponding sides are not, so the figures
are not congruent. **4.** rotation and translation;
congruent   **5.** $(-2, 1)$ **6.** $(-3, 3)$ **7.** $(-3, -3)$
8. $(-1, 2)$ **9.** $(-3, -4)$ **10.** $(2, 0)$ **11.** $(0, 3)$
12. $(5, 1)$ **13.** $(4, -3)$ **14.** $(2, 0)$ **15.** $(-3, 0)$
16. $(1, 5)$

Quiz

1. The figures are congruent because all pairs of
corresponding sides and all pairs of corresponding
angles are congruent. The reflection was a rigid
motion.   **2.** translation; left 3, down 5
3. reflection over x-axis   **4.** rotation; 90°
counterclockwise   **5.** translation; 3 left and 3
down OR 180° rotation   **6.** reflection over y-axis
7. translation 3 left

Answers continued

Benchmark 3

A. Special Segments in Triangles.

1. 10 **2.** 16 **3.** 8 **4.** 8 **5.** 16 **6.** 8

7. $(0, w)$ **8.** $\left(\dfrac{w}{2}, 2w\right)$ **9.** w **10.** $\dfrac{w}{2}$ **11.** $\dfrac{w\sqrt{5}}{2}$

12. $\overline{AC} \cong \overline{BC}$; $\overline{AD} \cong \overline{DB}$; $\overline{AM} \cong \overline{MB}$

13. $\triangle ACD \cong \triangle BCD$; SSS postulate. **14.** $x = \dfrac{9}{4}$

15. $y = \dfrac{9}{2}$ **16.** $z = 1$ **17.** $x = 6$

18. $x = 17$ **19.** $x = 3$ **20.** No **21.** $\left(\dfrac{1}{8}, 0\right)$

22. $(1,1)$ **23.** $(0, -4)$ **24.** $4\sqrt{3}$

25. $(2, 1)$ **26.** $(0, -1)$ **27.** $(1, 3)$ **28.** $(0, 1)$

29. Outside **30.** Outside **31.** Outside

32. Inside

Quiz

1. 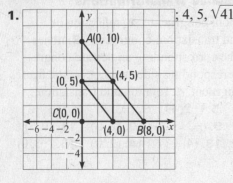 ; 4, 5, $\sqrt{41}$

2. $M\left(-\dfrac{a}{2}, \dfrac{b}{2}\right), N\left(\dfrac{a}{2}, \dfrac{b}{2}\right), a$ **3.** $x = 6$ **4.** $(0, 10)$

5. $(4, 4)$ **6.** $(0, 1)$

B. Inequalities in Triangles

1. $\angle A, \angle C, \angle B$ **2.** $\angle D, \angle F, \angle E$ **3.** $\overline{HI}, \overline{GH},$
$\overline{GI}$ **4.** $\overline{KL}, \overline{JK}, \overline{JL}$ **5.** $\angle M, \angle O, \angle N$

6. $\overline{QR}, \overline{PQ}, \overline{PR}$ **7.** Between 14 and 58 feet
8. Between 13 and 25 yards **9.** Between 1 and
5 inches **10.** Between 50 and 56 miles
11. Between 4 and 8 cm **12.** Between 19 and
33 m **13.** 8.5 miles **14.** B, D **15.** B **16.** D
17. B, C, A, D **18.** The angle opposite the longer
side of a triangle is smaller than the angle opposite
the shorter side. **19.** The side opposite the larger
angle of a triangle is shorter than the side opposite
the smaller angle. **20.** There are two sides in
a triangle the sum of whose lengths is less than
or equal to the length of the third side. **21.** The
included angle of the first triangle is smaller than
the included angle of the second.

Quiz

1a. longer than 4, shorter than 20 **1b.** longer
than 21, shorter than 49 **2a.** AC, BC, AB
2b. BC, AB, AC **3.** AD **4.** There are two odd
integers whose sum is not even.

C. Similarity and Proportionality Theorems

1. $x = \dfrac{24}{7}$; scale factor = 1.75 **2.** $x = 15$; scale
factor = 1.5 **3.** $x = \dfrac{90}{13}$; scale factor ≈ 0.77

4. $x = 10.2$; scale factor = 1.25 **5.** 40 inches

6. $\dfrac{H}{h} = \dfrac{S}{s}$ **7.** Yes. The same proportions apply.
The sun's angle is still the same for both triangles.

8. $\triangle LMN \sim \triangle RST$; $\triangle ABC \sim \triangle DEF$

9. 8, 10 **10.** $\dfrac{36}{7}, \dfrac{20}{7}$ **11.** 12, 15 **12.** 3, 5

13. $x = 9$ **14.** $x = 3$ **15.** $x = 3.2$ **16.** No
17. dilation with scale factor 3 **18.** dilation with
scale factor 15 **19.** dilation with center A and
scale factor $\dfrac{3}{2}$ **20.** $L(-6, 2), M(0, 4), N(4, -8)$
21. $L(1, -1), M(1.5, -1), N(-1, -2)$
22. $L(2, 1), M(1, 0), N(-3, 2)$ **23.** $L(25, -10),$
$M(35, -20), N(60, -30)$

24. $x = 6$ **25.** $x = 15$

26. $x = \dfrac{4}{3}$ **27.** $x = 3$ **28.** $AB = 15.2$

29. $AB = 2.4$ **30.** $AB = 9\sqrt{2}$

Quiz

1. $x = 10$, scale factor = 0.6 **2.** 3 feet 9 inches
3a. $\triangle ABC \sim \triangle ADE$ by the SSS Similarity
Theorem **3b.** $\triangle ABC \sim \triangle EDC$ by the SAS
Similarity Theorem **3c.** $\triangle ACE \sim \triangle BCD$ by the
AA Similarity Postulate

4. dilation with center C and scale factor 3

5.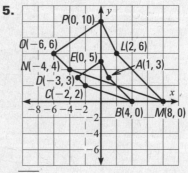

6. $\overline{AB} = 26$

D: Pythagorean Theorem and Right Triangles

1. hypotenuse; $x = \sqrt{97}$ **2.** leg; $x = 2\sqrt{26}$

3. hypotenuse; $x = \sqrt{113}$ **4.** leg; $x = 5$

5. $x = 60$ **6.** $x = 130$ **7.** $x = 125$ **8.** $x = 400$

9. acute   **10.** acute   **11.** obtuse   **12.** obtuse

13. $\triangle DAB \sim \triangle BAC \sim \triangle DBC$; $x = 4.8$

14. $\triangle HFG \sim \triangle HGE \sim \triangle GFE$; $x = \frac{120}{13} \approx 9.2$

15. $\triangle IKJ \sim \triangle ILK \sim \triangle JLK$; $x = 2\sqrt{2} \approx 2.8$

16. $\triangle MON \sim \triangle OPN \sim \triangle MPO$; $x = 10$

17. 9.91 feet   **18.** 8.26 feet   **19.** 7.40 feet

20. 10.52 feet   **21.** $x = \frac{9\sqrt{3}}{2}$; $y = \frac{9}{2}$

22. $x = 6\sqrt{3}$; $y = 12\sqrt{3}$

23. $x = 4\sqrt{3}$; $y = 4\sqrt{6}$ **24.** $x = 2\sqrt{2}$

Quiz

1a. leg; $x = 9\sqrt{3}$ **1b.** hypotenuse; $x = 57\sqrt{2}$

2. 72   **3a.** obtuse   **3b.** obtuse

4. $\triangle ACD \sim \triangle ABC \sim \triangle CBD$; $x = 24$

5. $\triangle DEG \sim \triangle EFG \sim \triangle DFE$; $x = \frac{64}{11}$

6. $\triangle HJI \sim \triangle IJG \sim \triangle GIH$; $x = 20$

7. $x = 18\sqrt{3}$, $y = 9$ **8.** $x = 18\sqrt{2}$, $y = 36$

E. Sine, Cosine, and Tangent

1. $\tan J = \frac{4}{3} \approx 1.3333$; $\tan K = \frac{3}{4} = 0.75$

2. $\tan J = \frac{24}{7} \approx 3.4286$; $\tan K = \frac{7}{24} \approx 0.2917$

3. $\tan J = 1$; $\tan K = 1$ **4.** $\tan J = \sqrt{3} \approx 1.7321$;
$\tan K = \frac{1}{\sqrt{3}} \approx 0.5774$ **5.** $x \approx 24.9$ **6.** $x \approx 14.3$

7. $x \approx 19.1$ **8.** $x \approx 8.9$

9. $\sin S = \frac{4}{5} = 0.8$; $\cos S = \frac{3}{5} = 0.6$

10. $\sin S = \frac{1}{2} = 0.5$; $\cos S = \frac{\sqrt{3}}{2} \approx 0.8660$

11. $\sin S = \cos S = \frac{\sqrt{2}}{2} \approx 0.7071$

12. $\sin S = \frac{7}{25} = 0.28$; $\cos S = \frac{24}{25} = 0.96$

13. $\ell \approx 16.2$ feet; $h \approx 15.4$ feet

14. $\ell \approx 64.7$ feet; $h \approx 61.6$ feet

15. $\ell \approx 12.4$ feet; $h \approx 7.3$ feet

16. $\ell \approx 24.7$ feet; $h \approx 14.5$ feet

17. The distance from the base of the ladder to the base of the building is half that or twice that as in the example, while the angle of elevation is the same. The length of the ladder and the height of the window is correspondingly half as much or twice as great.

18. No   **19.** 25.5°   **20.** 12.0°   **21.** 52.5°

22. 27.5°   **23.** 53.6°   **24.** 89.7°

25. 42°, 48°, 90°; 6.0, 6.7, 9

26. 23°, 67°, 90°; 16, 37.7, 40.9

27. 22°, 68°, 90°; 12, 29.7, 32.0

Quiz

1. 1.3333   **2.** 0.8000   **3.** 0.7500   **4.** 36.8700°

5. 53.1301°   **6.** 36.8700°   **7.** 41.2 feet

Benchmark 4

A. Parallelograms

1. 90°   **2.** 50°   **3.** 65°   **4.** 135°   **5.** 120°

6. 150°   **7.** 108°; 72°   **8.** 120°; 60°

9. 128.6°; 51.4°   **10.** 140°; 40°   **11.** 144°; 36°

12. 154.3°; 25.7°   **13.** $x = 120$; $y = 60$; $z = 8$

14. $x = 30$; $y = 3$; $z = 40$ **15.** $MQ = 3$

16. $MO = 6$ **17.** $m\angle PNO = 85°$

18. $m\angle MPO = 130°$ **19.** $m\angle NOP = 50°$

20. $PN = 4$ **21.** Theorem 8.8   **22.** Theorem 8.7

23. Theorem 8.10   **24.** Theorem 8.9

25. rhombus, square; In these parallelograms, all four sides are congruent. Therefore any two consecutive sides are congruent.   **26.** rhombus, square; In these parallelograms, each diagonal bisects each pair of opposite angles.

27. rectangle, square; In these parallelograms, the diagonals are congruent.   **28.** square; In a rhombus, the diagonals are perpendicular to each other. In a rectangle, the diagonals are congruent. Only a square is both a rhombus and a rectangle.   **29.** rectangle, square; In these parallelograms, all four angles are right angles. Therefore any two consecutive angles are congruent.   **30.** rectangle, rhombus, square; In any parallelogram, both pairs of opposite angles are congruent.

Quiz

1. 67°   **2.** 120°   **3.** $O(0, 0)$, $P(4, 0)$, $Q(0, 3)$, $R(-4, 3)$, $S(0, \frac{3}{2})$ **4.** Yes   **5.** No   **6.** No

7. No   **8.** No

B. Special Quadrilaterals

1. Yes   **2.** No   **3.** No   **4.** Yes   **5.** $m\angle B = 40°$, $m\angle C = 140°$, $m\angle D = 140°$, $AC = 7$, $MN = 5$

6. $m\angle B = 60°$, $m\angle C = 120°$, $m\angle D = 120°$, $AC = 9$, $MN = 5$ **7.** $m\angle B = 67°$, $m\angle C = 67°$, $m\angle D = 113°$, $AC = 140$, $MN = 75$

8. $m\angle H = 100°$ **9.** $m\angle H = 69°$

10. $\sqrt{29}$ and $\sqrt{74}$ **11.** $\sqrt{170}$ and $\sqrt{85}$

Answers *continued*

12. isosceles trapezoid   **13.** kite
14. quadrilateral   **15.** square

Quiz

1–3.

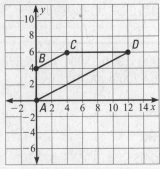

1. $\overline{BC} \parallel \overline{AD}$; $m = \frac{1}{2}$ **2.** No   **3.** $4\sqrt{5}$
4a. $x = 125$ **4b.** $x = 4$; $y = \sqrt{91}$ **5.** square

C. Translations

1. $(x, y) \rightarrow (x - 6, y - 2)$
2.

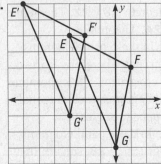

3. $(x, y) \rightarrow (x + 2, y - 3)$ **4.** $\overrightarrow{JK}\langle 3, 0\rangle$
5. $\overrightarrow{XY}\langle -5, 2\rangle$ **6.** $\overrightarrow{CD}\langle 0, -4\rangle$ **7.** $G'(-9, 0)$,
$R'(-2, 0)$, $A'(1, 6)$, $M'(-6, 6)$.
8. $X(7, 1)$, $Y(2, -4)$, $Z(5, -6)$ **9.** $\langle 7, 4\rangle$
10. $A'(-5, 6)$, $B'(-1, 6)$, $C'(-1, 4)$,
$D'(-5, 4)$ **11.** $\begin{bmatrix} -4 & -4 & -4 \\ -2 & -2 & -2 \end{bmatrix}$ **12.** $\begin{bmatrix} -4 & -2 \\ -7 & -2 \end{bmatrix}$

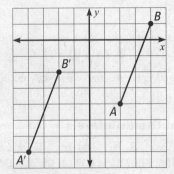

Quiz

1. $(x, y) \rightarrow (x - 3, y - 3)$ **2.** $\overrightarrow{LM}\langle 5, -3\rangle$
3. $R'(-2, 7)$, $S'(-1, 0)$, $T'(-6, -1)$ **4a.** $(-6, 5)$
4b. $(-1, -3)$ **5.** $\begin{bmatrix} -4 & -4 & -4 \\ -3 & -3 & -3 \end{bmatrix} + \begin{bmatrix} 5 & 4 & 1 \\ -2 & -8 & -3 \end{bmatrix}$
$= \begin{bmatrix} 1 & 0 & -3 \\ -5 & -11 & -6 \end{bmatrix}$

D. Reflections, Rotations, and Dilations

1. $M'(4, -1)$, $N'(2, -8)$ **2.** $M''(-2, -3)$, $N''(0, 4)$
3. $J'(-5, -2)$, $K'(1, 5)$ **4.** *slope of* $y = x$ *is* 1;
slope of $JJ' = \dfrac{-5 - (-2)}{-2 - (-5)} = \dfrac{-1}{1}$ **5.** $J''(5, 2)$,
$K''(-1, -5)$ **6.** $F'(-4, 2)$, $E'(1, -2)$, $D'(3, 3)$
7. $F''(4, -2)$, $E''(-1, 2)$, $D''(-3, -3)$
8–10. Check student graphs. Coordinates are given.
8. $S'(0, -5)$, $T'(-4, -2)$, $U'(2, 1)$
9. $S'''(5, 0)$, $T'''(2, -4)$, $U'''(-1, 2)$ **10.** $S''(0, 5)$,
$T''(4, 2)$, $U''(-2, -1)$ **11.** $T'(-2, 3)$, $U'(-5, 5)$,
$V'(-1, 6)$ **12.** $T''(2, -3)$, $U''(5, -5)$, $V''(1, -6)$
13. $T'''(3, 2)$, $U'''(5, 5)$, $V'''(6, 1)$ **14.** $M'(18, 15)$,
$N'(9, 6)$, $O'(3, 12)$ **15.** $B'(8, -4)$, $C'(-6, 6)$
16. $A''(-1, -2)$, $B''(1, -4)$, $C''(3, -1)$
17. $A''(-3, 1)$, $B''(-1, 3)$, $C''(-4, 5)$
18. $D''(-2, -3)$, $E''(-1, -6)$, $F''(-3, -7)$
19. $D''(-2, -4)$, $E''(-1, -1)$, $F''(-3, 0)$

Quiz

1. $R'(-5, 6)$, $S'(-3, 8)$ **2.** $R''(2, 5)$, $S''(4, 3)$
3. $G'(2, 4)$ **4.** $G''(-2, -4)$ **5.** $E'(0, -6)$,
$F'(6, 12)$, $G'(4, -2)$ **6.** $D'(-2, -5)$,
$E'(-4, -2)$

E. Symmetry

1. One line of symmetry   **2.** Five lines of
symmetry   **3.** Four lines of symmetry
4. One line of symmetry   **5.** Check student's
triangles–must be scalene triangle   **6.** No
7. Yes; 180°   **8.** Yes; 180°

Quiz

1.

Answers continued

2.

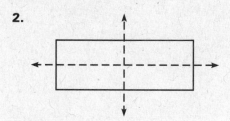

3. True   **4.** Yes

Benchmark 5

A. Circles and Special Segments

1. J **2.** $\overline{JK}$ or $\overline{JL}$ **3.** $\overline{LK}$ **4.** $\overline{KO}$ **5.** $\overrightarrow{KP}$
6. $\overleftrightarrow{MN}$ **7.** radius is 3 units   **8.** Yes, $6^2 + 8^2 = 10^2$
9. 7.2   **10.** 12   **11.** 18   **12.** 180°   **13.** 20°
14. 340°   **15.** 90°   **16.** 270°   **17.** 90°
18. 270°   **19.** $x = 58$ **20.** $SY = 8$
21.

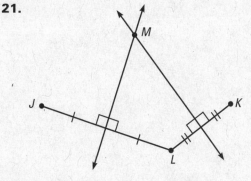

22. 12   **23.** 10.58   **24.** , 6   **25.** 2
26. $14\frac{1}{3}$ **27.** 4.7   **28.** 1.9   **29.** 32

Quiz

1. $\overline{LN}$ **2.** $\overline{KL}$ or $\overline{KJ}$ **3.** $\overleftrightarrow{OM}$ **4.** 9   **5.** 116°
6. 32°   **7.** 296°   **8.** 64°   **9.** 6   **10.** 2   **11.** 6
12. 10   **13.** 8

B. Angle Relationships in Circles

1. 35°   **2.** 100°   **3.** 34°   **4.** 68°   **5.** 18   **6.** 18
7. 40°   **8.** 212°   **9.** 115°   **10.** 48.5°   **11.** 18°
12. 78°   **13.** $(x + 1)^2 + (y - 2)^2 = 16$
14. $(x - 4)^2 + (y + 2)^2 = 36$ **15.** $x^2 + y^2 = 4$
16. $(x - 1)^2 + (y - 2)^2 = 52$

Quiz

1. 45°   **2.** 100°   **3.** 90.5°   **4.** 50°   **5.** 97°
6. $(x + 6)^2 + (y - 2)^2 = 36$

C. Circumference and Area of Circles

1. 31.42 feet   **2.** 40.84 yards   **3.** 113.10 miles
4. 5.34 mm   **5.** 0.64 miles   **6.** 1.43 meters
7. 0.25 inches   **8.** 1.59 units   **9.** 3.05 yards
10. 15.27 km   **11.** 79.85 feet

12. 3.14 light-years   **13.** 78.54 ft²
14. 132.73 yards²   **15.** 1017.88 miles²
16. 2.27 mm²   **17.** 1.13 miles
18. 1.69 m   **19.** 0.71 inches   **20.** 1.78
units   **21.** 44.68 units²   **22.** 11.31 units²
23. 134.04 units²   **24.** 6.28 units²
25. 26.18 units²   **26.** 76.97 units²

Quiz

1. 62.83 in.   **2.** 1.91 in.   **3.** area: 9.42 m²;
arclength: 3.14 m   **4.** 452.39 cm²   **5.** 1.95 cm
6. 12.28 cm

D. Solids

1. Yes, it is a triangular prism. 5 faces, 6 vertices,
9 edges.   **2.** Yes, it is a polyhedron, but it is
neither a prism nor a pyramid. 5 faces, 6 vertices,
9 edges.   **3.** Yes, it is a trapezoidal prism. 6 faces,
8 vertices, 12 edges.   **4.** Yes, it is a trapezoidal
pyramid. 5 faces, 5 vertices, 8 edges.   **5.** $5 + 6 =$
$9 + 2$ **6.** $5 + 6 = 9 + 2$ **7.** $6 + 8 = 12 + 2$
8. $5 + 5 = 8 + 2$ **9.** a circle   **10.** an ellipse
11. an equilateral triangle   **12.** a square
13. $S_1 = 181.33$ cm², $V_1 = 772.74$ cm³
14. $S_1 = 1988.17$ m², $V_1 = 20304.05$ m³
15. $S_1 = 896$ in.², $V_1 = 5696$ in.³
16. $S_1 = 36$ miles², $V_1 = 373.36$ miles³

Quiz

1. $F = 8, E = 18, V = 12$ **2.** $F = 11, E = 20,$
$V = 11$ **3.** Point, square, rectangle, equilateral
triangle, isosceles triangle, scalene triangle
4a. $2 : 3$ **4b.** 900

E: Spheres, Pyramids, and Cones

1. $r = 4.51$ cm   **2.** $r = 15.58$ m
3. $S = 4536.46$ in.²   **4.** $S = 124.03$ yds²
5. $S = 1.77$ miles²   **6.** $r = 0.5$ feet
7. 10 cm³   **8.** 7 ft³   **9.** 62.20 mm³
10. 4289.32 m³   **11.** 9 in.³   **12.** 129.88 units³
13. 33.51 ft³   **14.** 696.91 in.³   **15.** 1047.39 mm³
16. 129.88 miles³   **17.** 904,778,684.2 cm³
18. 1,563,457.57 m³

Quiz

1. $\sqrt{6}$ units

2. 56 units³

3. 44.60 cm²

4. 5.83 m

Answers continued

Benchmark 6

A. Probabilities of Simple and Compound Events

1. $\frac{3}{20}$ **2.** $\frac{3}{10}$ **3.** $\frac{7}{20}$ **4.** $\frac{1}{5}$ **5.** $1 : 25, 25 : 1$

6. $1 : 12, 12 : 1$ **7.** $1 : 3, 3 : 1$ **8.** $3 : 10,$
$10 : 3$ **9.** 6 **10.** 360 **11.** 24 **12.** 5040

13. 15 **14.** 56 **15.** 5 **16.** 210 **17.** $\frac{2}{3}$

18. $\frac{2}{3}$ **19.** $\frac{5}{6}$ **20.** $\frac{1}{12}$ **21.** $\frac{5}{33}$ **22.** $\frac{5}{44}$

Quiz

1. $\frac{1}{5}$ **2.** $\frac{2}{15}$ **3.** $\frac{1}{3}$ **4.** $\frac{1}{15}$ **5.** $1 : 12, 12 : 1$

6. $1 : 51, 51 : 1$ **7.** $1 : 25, 25 : 1$ **8.** $9 : 4,$
$4 : 9$ **9.** 12 **10.** 60 **11.** 24 **12.** 2520

13. 10 **14.** 15 **15.** 55 **16.** 35 **17.** $\frac{5}{6}$ **18.** $\frac{2}{3}$

19. $\frac{7}{64}$ **20.** $\frac{1}{12}$ **21.** $\frac{1}{12}$